We're F*cked

Realizing potential, not maximizing wealth, military power, or social control is how we'll survive this century

By Peter Nixon, FCPA

Testimonials for the pre-publication edition of this book

Evelyn Tong	Zhong Lun Law Firm	It is inevitable to work with clients and staff in a single jurisdiction nowadays. Understand how to build good cross-cultural communications is key to maintain a business's competitive edge, build stronger bonds with clients and staff and improve productivity.
Denis Vaillancourt	Securicom Solutions	Cultural differences can be an impediment to constructive dialogue. Peter's book will help us find a solution to that problem by analysing the root causes and overcoming the hurdles.
Yoosuf	CCL	For better understanding and reflections on impact
Veronique Lafon-Vinais	HKUST	In a world where Trump leads the US, we need more understanding of what various cultures bring to the table
Dasu Ram Parajuli	Nepal Chamber of Commerce Hong Kong	Read & assess the positive factors of the book.
Niels Kraunsoe	Niels Kraunsoe - Facilitator and Mediator	I spent most of career straddling two quite different cultures, Chinese and English. I firmly believe that cultural factors and their understanding is key to success in any enterprise. This was very obvious of my own field of managing major construction projects. Peter Nixon is an experienced and clear thinker in this field and I believe that this book will add to the important body of relevant knowledge and experience.
Diane Long	Fidelity International	Culture is a key factor in the success of a company!
Case Everaert	Black Isle Group	Because Culture is a lot more tangible than people think. It needs to be worked on, bit by bit and day by day.
Lawrence Law	Standard Chartered Bank	Working in a multicultural work environment, it is essential to understand the differences in work culture and leadership.
Florent BUIRON	TEAM POTENTIAL	The world is turning increasingly complex through a variety of factors (technology, demographics, politics -hey we got our lot lately !-), and crucially, the independencies and systemic angle is often overlooked by leaders in how to grapple with challenges, whether they are business, sociological, or political challenges. Overcoming cultural differences and building common cultural foundations or reference points around which to anchor our action is clearly key. I think your book is very timely!! Well done, by the way. Never an easy endeavour to write a book like this.
Lily Lau	Culture Dynamics Malaysia	Culture is the foundation to different understanding of how underlying assumptions, expectations, what should and should not in. Understanding of culture will help to break barriers and build bridges to overcome differences.
Yu Joseph	Roseville group	With globalization and Internet communication, a revisit of their impact on cultural challenges and indeed leadership styles is necessary.

Robert Lamoureux	CIT Aerospace	Peter has made a significant contribution in my team negotiation strategies and i am curious to discover his wisdom on cultural hurdles.
Dittmar Nerger	Nerger Consulting Co. Ltd.	Understanding a partner's culture can "make or break" a business relationship. Ignorance of culture can make a negotiation painful and fail. Understanding and overcoming cultural hurdles instead can turn confrontation into dialogue, frustration into success. Critical learning to prepare for a meeting, for a foreign assignment, to understand your partner and yourself for mutual benefit.
Hui Tung wai	Concerto Capital	Peter negotiation class helps.
Kersten hui	Infinity equity	Peter class of how different people negotiate has big impact on my day to day operation.
Daniel Chan	HKJC	Culture difference can make or break any business
Regina Chu	InterContinental Hong Kong	This is a diversified workplace.
William Du	New World Development	The book is a timely call at this era of global uncertainty to look more at cultural elements of business in order to have the business savvy contextually fit for a particular locality.
G Tan	freelance	Culture is like the air we breathe.
Rajeev Kumar	Tata Services	can submit after reading through the book
Bob Griffith	Lions International	Curious
pascale	Equoranda	I facilitate many seminars in multinational companies to create "cultures" that help in these complex times. So, I am curious to discover the 9 cultural hurdles
Evan Price	CO2 Solutions	I am most interested in reading Peter's next book and a subject that is very topical in today's environment.
John Mavridis	CMKZ, Newhouse and the Mark McLaughlin Fan Club	In a world that interconnects, I need to read the insight of a professional whose work spans borders and has the discipline to think and share his thoughts about the impact of Culture in business.
Marsha Hanna	Sotheby's	I would like to read this book as communication is how we survive.
Marvin Lim	Barnes Aerospace	New perspective
Vic Lindal	Coach	Globalization
Eric Goujon	PricewaterhouseCoopers Zhong Tian LLP Beijing Branch	Culture (of a people, country, or organisation) is what drives behaviours, beliefs and reactions to events. Not to apprehend the cultural features, not to integrate them into the analysis and decision-making process is likely to result at best in inefficiencies, at worst in destructive measures. Conversely, while apprehension might not grant understanding, it can at least make people of different cultures interacting together a happier experience. And that is already a feast in itself.
Andrew Willis		The leading economies of the future will be the most culturally diverse. The most successful businesses of the future will be the product of cross-cultural synergies that only increase in efficacy, benefitting from a wider array of strategies and best practices.

Kingsley Smith	Mda	Because no one has a handle on this subject! It is probably the biggest gap in most international executives' skillset - effectively dealing with people from other cultures.
Philip Purver	TheWorkingManager	Greater competition from countries around the world means that understanding culture and country market approach is more critical than ever.
Zeph Koay	Independent Consultant	Doing business across borders is challenging in itself, and the diversity of cultures across many boarders poses added challenges that needed to be overcome. This book which shows us ways to overcome these challenges is therefore of much value to readers who are involve with doing business in a global economy.
Azham	Razak School of Government	Better understanding on important elements that are taken granted by many nations and organizations.
Anonymous		Some emerging economies will forever be emerging unless they get the culture right. It starts at the top.

Other Books by Peter Nixon

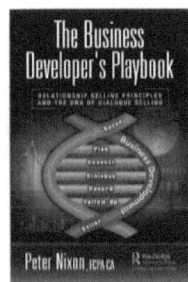

Praise for *The Business Developers Playbook*

"This book is an absolute must read. It is not a book about selling in the limited way we generally think of that word, it is about influencing outcomes and making a difference, both to your life and success, and to the lives of others". Robin Stuart-Kotze, author of *The Seven Secrets of Highly Effective Leaders*

Praise for *Dialogue Gap*

"Dialogue Gap is a timely call for all of us who care for the fate of humanity's future. I urge everyone who is concerned about the health of humanity and the world we live in to read this important book". Thupten Jinpa, English translator to the Dalai Lama and author of Essential Mind Training

Praise for *Negotiation: Mastering Business in Asia*

"This book gives practical solutions to challenges and dilemmas encountered in the business arena, social scene and cross-cultural environment. I am sure this comprehensive negotiation toolkit will be especially useful to people at all levels in different disciplines, particularly for those eyeing the markets of Asia". Loretta Ho, Director HKRI

Publisher

Potential Limited, Suite 4e Brilliance, Discovery Bay, Hong Kong

Dedication

I dedicate this book to Ni Si, Long Tim, and Jean-Pierre, who despite the odds, became my children and who together with their cousins, friends, and peers around the world, will overcome the today's challenges of climate change, over population and pandemics to achieve optimal outcomes @work, @home and @large in their communities. Good luck, work hard, have faith, and remember:

"You want to succeed,
and you will.
Manage talent, training, time,
money, energy, and people.
Most important of all,
Learn to control your emotions
to enhance your situation
rather than hinder it."

Table of Contents

Preface

Is the world lost? Consider the health of the world's population, the world's economy or the world's climate and I think you have your answer. Coronavirus forced us all to press the pause button at the start of 2020. Here in Hong Kong the slowdown started earlier than in Western countries and thankfully led to a much flatter curve of infections. Following this long period of social distancing and cancelled events, time has provided a chance to reflect on three things: **the world's interconnectedness** made obvious by the speed of the pandemic spread; **things for which we are grateful** e.g. healthcare; and **things we wish to correct** like climate change, the recession and bad governance.

In terms of interconnectedness the pandemic has already infected tens of millions of people and caused hundreds of thousands of deaths. The lockdown has bankrupted industries, escalated conflicts, and strained relationships. Some leaders have failed to see or accept the unexpected consequences of the pandemic while others, not happy with the implications, have nonetheless responded by learning what to do and just doing it e.g. cancel gatherings and wear a mask.

As we watch our news feeds on our phones and computers headlines have been particularly full of bad news, some of which has sadly affected us and our families directly. Despite this or possibly because of it, we have been buoyed by the frontline workers who have continued to provide the essential services and kept things going while most others remain locked down and out of work. For this we are grateful.

This long break has also enabled us to focus on the things that need fixing, the climate, the economy, and bad governance. These three problems affect all of us to a greater or lesser extent. The purpose of this book is to describe the new direction that is needed, to stress we are all in this together, and to highlight the common hurdles which more successful leaders, organisations and nations are overcoming today (in my experience) to achieve optimal outcomes despite our common problems.

I refer to **nine behaviours**, or hurdles which we must overcome to achieve our new **one economic goal** of achieving optimal outcomes defined as realizing our potential while helping others realise theirs. I was born a late baby boomer but opted instead to live a very different lifestyle which afforded me the opportunity to work with thousands of leaders in hundreds of organisations in 60 countries around the world.

When the pandemic shut down travel globally and put an end over thirty years of monthly travel, it gave me a unique opportunity to reflect on my experience, develop my online courses, and put the finishing touches on this book which had been in development for some time.

Moving all of my work online meant that I was transitioning from boomer to zoomer. I am pleased to offer my insights in these pages and welcome to engage with me online to figure out how to apply these in your specific situation.

Leaders want their organisations and governments to jump the hurdles as quickly as possible to achieve an optimal outcome for themselves and their stakeholders, be they employees, shareholders, or citizens. The economic theory driving this behaviour is called *Potentialism*. It suggests "we have a duty to realise our potential while helping others realise theirs". Leaders, organisations, and nations that will flourish in the 21st century will be those that put achieving potential, not maximizing profits, or maintaining social control as the primary motivation of their behaviours.

The 2020s is a decade of decisions because we all need to learn to live together peacefully and sustainably better than ever before. I highlight **020** or "O to O" because the 2020s is also the first decade where we must learn to live successfully both online and offline (i.e. O to O) in other words, we all have to learn to live as comfortably on the internet as we live off the internet. Given the pervasive nature of the internet today we have no choice but to live in both the virtual world and (as the Urban dictionary calls it "IRL") in real life.

The nine hurdles which are slowing leaders from achieving potential have mostly emerged since the internet of things took precedence around the year 2000 followed by the collapse of the world economy in 2008. This latest pandemic has simply reinforced these hurdles. To remember the hurdles, just say: "Inspiration STOPs BAD Faith" and you will remember all nine.

Successful leaders today create **inspiration** in their followers because of the positive changes they have created through innovation and entrepreneurship. They have acted with respect to both **sustainability** and **trusteeship** and in doing so became beacons for environmentalists and investors. Their **openness** to diversity and new ways of **partnering** have enabled start-ups to win while less agile organisations go bankrupt or are bought out by new investors. These 21st century leaders also show **bravery, alertness** to change and a willingness to **dialogue** amongst key stakeholders thereby enabling them to stay abreast of rapid change while their competitors possibly less skilled or willing get tripped up by the same hurdles and fall behind. Finally, an old world favourite brought back into vogue by the death and instability caused by this global pandemic, a leader's **faith**, regardless of where it is derived, is an ingredient of great leaders who know, sooner or later, if they follow these behaviours in their quest to realise their potential while helping others realise theirs, they will either succeed sooner or learn from their mistakes and to succeed later.

The mnemonic "Inspiration STOPs BAD Faith" causes people to ask me what I mean by bad faith. I refer to three types of bad faith:
1) following a leader in or out of a crisis just because he or she is your leader can cause you or your organisation your life. Many leaders today are lost and simply collecting huge salaries without really knowing how to change.
2) joining a big name organisation because you think it is a safe job when many of the most established organsations are disappearing or being surpassed by previously unknown competitors.
3) thinking you can get better results by doing the same thing faster when in many cases people are simply doing the wrong thing.

If the massive changes caused by the pandemic have caused you or your organisation to lose direction, all you need to do is recalibrate your compass by engaging in dialogue with your key stakeholders to clarify your potential and get working together to jump the various hurdles in your way. It is only in doing this together can you achieve your potential while helping others realise theirs.

This book is an easy read full of plenty of anecdotes derived from my boomer to zoomer existence. The various hurdles will become well known to you and I hope through reading and reflecting on these hurdles you will be able to identify which are you back from realizing your potential.

Good luck in this pandemic. Remember, the solution is in the dialogue, so contact me if you get stuck.

Peter Nixon, July 2020
Discovery Bay, Hong Kong
www.PotentialDialogue.com

Introduction

"Hire not on cultural fit, but on cultural contribution.
When leaders prize cultural fit, they end up hiring people who think in similar ways.
Originality comes not from people who match the culture, but from those who enrich it.
Before interviews, identify the diverse backgrounds, skill sets, and personality traits
that are currently missing from your culture.
Then place a premium on those attributes in the hiring process". (Grant)

I grew up in English-speaking Montreal in the 1960's singing *God Save the Queen* at Carlyle School. Just that is enough to tell you I am an English-speaking baby boomer. By the age of six my family and I were celebrating with the rest of the world at Montreal's 1967 world fair. At that time, I had no idea that the winds of change were approaching to cause the biggest changes to my culture since my ancestors moved to Lower Canada (later the Province of Quebec) in the early 1800's. Within ten short years Quebec separatists had gained power in Quebec and the English community began its fifty-year exodus out of what was then Canada's #1 city.

The English departed the Province Quebec mostly westward with their culture, industriousness and global networks to Toronto, Calgary, Vancouver and beyond. Once settled into their new communities they partnered with local leaders and helped grow these cities into the modern cities they are today. Meanwhile Montreal, the once grand dame of Canada, had fallen in many peoples' minds to fourth place in Canada. English businesses, schools, hospitals, clubs, community, and social institutions that were at one time first world examples of innovation and success, had closed, merged, or fallen into mismanagement.

Montreal's unnatural decline came during one of the world's most historic periods of growth. So why do some organisations, communities and nations attract and grow while others decline and fall behind? What differentiates leaders from laggards? Are there cultural elements consistent to those who succeed today? In this book I suggest that indeed there are cultural hurdles that leaders overcome and which hold others back. In this way I even suggest some emerging economies will never actually ever emerge.

After graduating from Bishop's University in Quebec's beautiful Eastern Townships I joined Canada's leading accounting firm, Coopers & Lybrand, in their bilingual Montreal office where years before the Montreal partners of MacDonald Currie (as the firm was originally known) were responsible for bringing together Coopers (from the UK) and Lybrand (from the US) to create the world's leading "Big 8" accountancy firm. Canadians united the British and Americans. Thirty years later Coopers & Lybrand merged with another Big 8 firm, Price Waterhouse, to create what is regarded by some, as the #1 firm worldwide and a leading member of the "Big 4". Despite this illustrious history the Montreal office of PwC is of little significance today in the scope of the global firm and despite being an alumnus of the Montreal, Geneva and Hong Kong offices, I feel less affinity to PwC because its culture is not that of C&L which I joined in 1983 and left ten years later after an enriching international audit career.

Change affects communities, companies, and individuals.   Having begun my career as a chartered accountant and auditor in Montreal, my career today sees me based in Hong Kong and consulting globally on dialogue, negotiation, and development. The most common question I am asked everywhere I go is:

"How did you transform from bean counter to international negotiator?"

After twenty-five years of consulting, 600+ engagements and 60+ countries, I am ready to venture an answer to this question. What people are usually asking when they ask for my story is how can they realise their story. The purpose of this book, building on my previous books on dialogue, negotiation and business development, is to give you, your organisations and your nation 1) some ideas to overcome the cultural hurdles which are slowing success and 2) provide you with tips to help develop your full potential. I believe we have a duty to realise our potential while helping others realise theirs. I call this Potentialism and it inspires my work daily. I explain more about this at the end of this book.

The pandemic has changed the world dramatically but even before the pandemic and resulting economic collapse, the world had already changed dramatically over the last fifty years. World population has doubled and at present there are some 65 million migrants in transit from their home country seeking safety and welfare in developed countries. Everyone in the world today has a family story of migration either recent or at some point in history. My ancestors, which I have traced as far back as 1548 (see About Author), left England, Ireland and Scotland at various points in the 17th, 18th and 19th centuries in hope of finding a better life in the "new world". One ancestor, Stephen Hopkins, famously arrived in America with his family on the Mayflower in 1620. All my ancestors travelled by ship and mostly landed in Montreal which was the most important port in British North America at that time. As people migrated from all over the world and landed in their new world they grouped together with people from their culture and looked after each other by building social and commercial institutions, trading and intermarrying thereby carrying on their traditions from the "old world".

Now, hundreds of years later, population growth and social integration means that we no longer live in our English, French or Chinese enclaves. Instead we live, study and work intermingled with people from all over the world. My wife is French Canadian of French and Irish descent. Two of my children are Chinese.   Globalisation and technological change have completely changed economies, jobs, where we live, and what we aspire to do.

The pandemic and racial protests notwithstanding, despite today's social integration (referred to as inter-culturalism, an upgrade on the multi-culturalism of the 1960's), people are still wondering how to get ahead socially and economically. Massive migration, political changes and dysfunctional leaders are all a result of the massive changes in the world today.   Every generation does what is necessary to improve the future for their children. What were the cultural elements of success that drew our ancestors to the "new world" hundreds of years ago and which still draw millions of migrants today? What are the cultural hurdles that have been overcome by leading countries but are still holding back failing states which are sadly losing their cherished sons and daughters to either covid'19 or better economies far away?

Back in the 1960's the students in my primary school (Carlyle School, Town of Mount Royal) were for the most part English speaking, protestant and white. My children's' schools (Discovery Bay International School and West Island School in Hong Kong) included classmates from multiple language groups, races, and religions. While I was studying in my homogeneous school environment in Montreal, a Dutch researcher was investigating cultural differences amongst employees at IBM. Geert Hofstede realised that if IBM were to become successful selling and servicing computer systems around the world, the company would need to learn how to work successfully across cultures. Even though IBM was a global company by the start of WWII, IBM's office environment in the 1960's was very much like my primary school with each location relatively homogenous. Today, regardless of which country you consider, IBM's workforce is now as culturally, racially, and linguistically diverse as my children's international schools.

Hofstede's cultural dimensions theory describes national cultures along six dimensions: Power Distance, Individualism, Uncertainty Avoidance, Masculinity, Long Term Orientation, and Indulgence vs. Restraint. His book, *Culture's Consequences,* became required reading for managers in the 20st century.

The world today is dramatically different than it was in the 1960's when Hofstede wrote his book. Hofstede's cultural differences, while interesting, are less relevant today than they were then. New cultural markers are needed to better understand differences in our inter-cultural world. To complicate things further, ask yourself, what culture are we today? I for example, grew up in an English Protestant world but half my life has now been lived in an expatriate community in Confucian Cantonese speaking Hong Kong, married to a French-Canadian Catholic, working across the world and in my spare time studying Buddhist philosophy and listening to classic rock played by my favourite Pilipino musicians and surfing online with friends and readers from around the world.

My inter-cultural lifestyle is not much different from other people I have worked with. Vivienne for example is ethnically Chinese, lives in a German family, was educated in England and brought up in Indonesia. Victor, who grew up in Hong Kong, emigrated to Australia and has lived there for so long he has an Aussie accent when he speaks English. We all have examples of friends, neighbours and family members who fit easily into more than one cultural description so our cultural descriptors need refining. My son described going to university in my hometown of Montreal as being on exchange because he was born and grew up in Hong Kong.

Reflecting on my experience advising executives, organisations, and governments internationally, I offer the cultural hurdles outlined in this book for separating today's leaders and laggards in terms of career, business, and nation building. Although academic research is needed to prove and refine these cultural hurdles, if you are looking for a quick understanding of cultural differences to forecast success, you are welcome to use these to colour and shape your own cultural paradigm.

I refer to my cultural descriptors as hurdles because they slow leaders down or trip them up before they learn how to overcome them (provided they want to make the effort to learn how). For some these hurdles remain impassable and will prevent certain organisations and nations from ever fully emerging. Each of the hurdles are described in the following chapters. You can read the chapters in any order you please. Before introducing the cultural hurdles please accept my definition of culture:

Culture is the ideas, customs, and behaviour of people in each space and time.

I like this definition because it reminds us that culture changes with space and time. The pandemic is rapidly changing culture. This is how the same culture can be different in two places at the same time e.g. a Chinese family run business in HK versus a Chinse run business in America or Chinese kids' vs their parents in Hong Kong today.

Here is another definition of culture which reinforces my nine cultural hurdles included in this book.

> "Cultures are defensive constructions against chaos,
> designed to reduce the impact of randomness on experience.
> They are adaptive responses, just as feathers are for birds and fur is for mammals.
> Cultures prescribe norms, evolve goals, build beliefs that help us
> tackle the challenges of existence.
> In so doing they must rule out many alternative goals and beliefs,
> and thereby limit possibilities, but this channelling of attention to a limited set of goals
> and means is what allows effortless action within self-created boundaries." (Csikszentmihalyi)

In my experience the cultural hurdles which I describe in this book transcend time and space and give us useful differentiators between the winners and losers in our interconnected pandemic world today. While individuals, companies and nations all strive for success and have hard work, sacrifice, focus and innovation, in common, the cultural hurdles I describe here differentiate the winners and losers by clarifying which stumble where thereby holding them back from achieving optimal outcomes.

Inspired
We love being inspired and when working with inspiration time flies. Our challenge is to find inspiration, team with others similarly inspired and sustain inspiration over time as things change and challenges are accomplished. In this chapter I share several examples of both inspired and uninspired leaders, companies, and nations. Individuals like NGO leader Bunker Roy or Tony, the printer cartridge salesman, change the world through their inspiration. Companies like Disney, which leverage people's inspiration, sustain success over decades by continuously tapping into the stream of inspiration. At the national level, politics by their very nature tap inspiration but things do not always work as we hope and I draw on examples from China, Burma, and Canada to make this obvious.

Sustainable
Sustainability requires systems (e.g. performance management, financial controls, training & development, succession planning) and pacing to enable leaders, companies, and nations to win continuously over the long term. In this chapter I offer interesting examples from Canada, Hong Kong, China, Iran, Thailand, and historic events of the last twenty years such as the collapse of the Berlin Wall, Hong Kong's handover to China and serving the 1%.

Trusteeship

The practice of trusteeship, protecting and enhancing assets before giving trusteeship of them to the next generation, used to be more common than today where people everywhere seem to enrich themselves almost hedonistically at the cost of future generations. In this chapter I share the work of inspiring leaders, companies and countries that are focused on winning over the long term and not simply meeting their quarterly profit requirements set by their stock market analysts. Examples come from hospitals, palm oil, UNICEF, family businesses, and camping.

Openness

Successful people today are also open to diverse ideas and concepts. Gone are the days of monotone audio and black and white video. Life today features high definition sound and colour. Rather than everyone thinking, doing, and dressing the same, most people now think, dress and act in a variety of ways making the new world of the 21st century far more interesting but also a lot more complicated. Until you learn to rejoice in and leverage diversity it can be scarily unfamiliar. There is a push back against diversity today for that very reason but to succeed today you need to be open to the full range of sights, sounds and colours that are swirling around you. Since organisations operate in highly volatile markets we need to stay tuned to diverse perspectives because this provides our competitive edge and ability to manage risks arising unexpectedly in our markets. Openness to and engagement with diversity at work, at home and in society will also allow us to attract and develop talent and innovation rather than drive it away to more open markets. In this chapter examples arise from home, work and international experience including wealth management, procurement, technological change and more.

Partnership

People, organisations, and nations that partner effectively with others achieve greater outcomes as compared to those which remain isolated in their silos or behind their fences without regard to the synergies awaiting them by joining others. Examples flow from politics, companies, universities, the Olympics and even taxes. We want to deal with conflict but cut off those who differ with us. Fuller success arises from learning to partner with key stakeholders despite their differences.

Bravery

Inspired, passionate, aligned people also bring a greater level of courage and bravery to their work. Feeling valued and doing something valuable means that when they encounter a hurdle standing in their way, inspired people are more courageous than the average to confront challenges and rectify the situation. Their bravery comes from a self-knowing and faith that stands firm and offers them a better option than bending or retreating in the face of hurdles. None of us start out brave. We learn through experience that most times when we push beyond our comfort zone the result is positive. Our economic system is based on the risk/reward trade-off so how can we develop bravery or work effectively in situations where a lack of courage prevails? In this chapter I draw on examples of leaders, companies, and nations that chose bravery or which shied away due to fear of the consequences. You read about people who kept to their beliefs and won in politics, business, and life despite the pain at the time.

Alert

Dynamic change and information overload necessitate successful leaders to remain alert by maintaining their mindfulness on the people and issues affecting them while also maintaining an inner calm and readiness to handle problems as they arise. Collectively, mindful leaders create mindful organisations and mindful communities which help ensure decisions and actions are taken cognizant of the reality in which they operate. In this chapter I share examples in music, big business and in society where mindfulness was lost or maintained and the results these brought. I also point to solutions for those wondering how to maintain their focus through complexity today.

Dialogue

Effective leaders, organisations, and nations also dialogue effectively internally and externally. In doing so they learn about the issues affecting them sooner, they learn to relate to stakeholders better and they respond effectively to the dynamic consequence impacting their situations. People in dialogue are better aware of what is going on and can adjust accordingly to sustain success over time. In this chapter I share a variety of examples from the leaders, companies, and communities I have been pleased to work with. Some of the stories have positive outcomes and some not so positive. Given rising conflict and increasing speed of change it is only dialogue, not the latest APP, which works fast enough to keep you on the winning side.

Faith

The central hurdle towards which the eight other hurdles point is that of faith and optimism. Leaders, companies, and nations that succeed over time are also those that sustain their faith in the face of opposition and who remain optimistic even in the face of setback. In this chapter I discuss a variety of examples arising from the depth of problems but which, like a lotus flower, start in the mud but eventually lead to a flowering of success.

Potentialism

I wrote this book to share my perception of the cultural hurdles differentiating successful leaders, organisations, and nations today. Challenged by the pandemic and facing seriously disrupted economies and supply chains, I have also included more thinking about potentialism, a subject I have touched upon in my earlier books as well. By putting potential at the heart of your economic policies, you will be more successful than focusing on profits or social control. My anecdotes come from both before and after the pandemic. We may never travel again like we did before the pandemic and without having travelled as I did, I may never have discovered these hurdles. Zoom is good but nothing beats being on site. When we anyone get to travel so much again?

It is clear to me, given my travels, that personal, corporate, ethnic, and national cultures are the differentiators between the best (companies and economies) and the rest. Culture differentiates leaders, their organisations, and nations. I touch upon all three levels, individual, organisational, and national, and provide anecdotes for each of these when discussing each of the hurdles blocking you from succeeding.

I adapted the Dharma Wheel icon, recognised by half the world population, to capture nine hurdles and potentialism (the jewel in the middle). The Dharma wheel or dharma chakra, as it is more widely known in the Hindu, Buddhist, and Jain religions, is an ancient symbol. Dharma (a Sanskrit word) means to hold, maintain, or keep that which is established or firm (like a trustee). Chakra derives from Indian and European languages including Greek, Slavic, and English. Chakra means to turn the wheel, cycle, or circle. Dharma chakras typically have eight, twelve or twenty-four spokes. The flag of India includes the Dharma Chakra and its 24 spokes tell the story of virtues shared in ancient Hindu Vedas. The ancient Kingdoms of Sikkim and Siam use eight spokes to represent the Buddhist Eightfold Path which leads from understanding to enlightenment. The twelve spoked dharma wheels commonly seen in Thailand today refers to the chain of dependant origination (the cycle of how things come to be, are and cease to be). I chose this symbol because I find it beautifully links the DNA double helix, from my *Business Developer's Playbook* with the cultural hurdles described herein.

In the following chapters, you will find each of the cultural hurdles described with individual, organisational, and national anecdotes drawn from my work and life history. It is not surprising that the culture of a company or nation is the consolidation of the people populating its leadership positions. In my experience culture begins with the individual and builds to organisations, communities, nations, and even world culture.

Given the economic collapse caused by the pandemic, a lot of people ask me career development questions. If they need a job, they ask for contacts but if they have a job they ask about the future:

- Should I get broad or deep experience, become a specialist or a generalist?

- Should I get local and international experience or just stay local?
- Should I push to get promoted or be wary about raising my head above the crowd for fear of having it cut off?

This book provides readers with plenty of career development tips and anecdotes to let you take your own decisions about your career because your personal situation is unique and there are no uniquely correct answers to the above questions. I hope you find this useful. In my career, after five years in Canada I moved overseas to gain international experience. After I had specialised in audit, I refined my specialisation to dialogue, negotiation, and development.

In the global economy post pandemic the more international experience you can accumulate, and the more the market recognises you as a specialist, the easier it will be for you to sell your skills be it locally or internationally. As for getting promoted, seldom will others champion your cause. Most cultures value understated expertise so if the people who need you can find you then it is better to be humble, otherwise speak up.

I hope you find my anecdotes valuable. If you are interested in learning more about dialogue, negotiation, or business development, I recommend you read my other books. This book joins the series and further defines the optimal outcome which appears in all my books.

I welcome your questions. Namaste _()_

Peter Nixon

Inspired

Unmotivated	Invigorating
Bureaucratic	Enthusiastic
Misdirected	Aligned

"Transformative leaders serve a transcendent purpose,
pointing the way to a new reality." (Goleman)

Individual

I was recently told by my graphic designer that I was only one of two deeply passionate clients they work with. As it turns out the other was also male with plenty of years behind him like me. What is less obvious, and I don't know the other gentleman, is that we are likely perceived as very passionate about our work because we have been lucky enough to end up doing what we love and loving what we do. I am grateful for having "found my calling" and that the market is willing to pay me to do it. As a result, I get to do more of what I love and less of what I do not although every job has its downside. I worked for a decade as an auditor and as long as I was learning new things, working with new clients and seeing new parts of the world I didn't mind doing the "grunt work" of long hours examining substantive evidence to prove or correct the figures in a company trial balance so that we could produce true and fair financial statements and attest to their correctness.

Inspiration involves a lot of things and if you are looking for inspiration in your work it is important that you try a lot of different things because it is only in widening your experience that you will find out what you don't like, what others find you to be talented at and what you find more enjoyable spending most your life doing. Until you find inspiration in your work, you will be bored and check the clock until finish time after which you can get onto what you really like to do. Since you spend a lot more of your waking hours at work than you do at home, Snow White and the Seven Dwarfs remind us to whistle on the way to work, not on the way home.

I love working with entrepreneurs and self-employed consultants because like artists and musicians they bring a passion to their work that far exceeds what I experience working with employees in large organisations. These people have a passion for what they do because they have chosen to do what they love. While overcoming all the economic barriers in the way of the self-employed, they like I, compare this work with the alternative of being an uninspired employee helping someone else pursue their dream and instead we push on towards our own goals.

Employees can be passionate too. If you are in a job that you love and find it possible to work endless hours without complaining, you too have experienced "flow" or peak experience where doing what you love and loving what you do enables you to do it over long periods of time without even realising how much time has actually transpired since you began. It is common to hear stories of such people setting alarms to remind themselves to stand up, drink water, eat lunch etc. because they are so into their work and so focused it is not uncommon for six hours to pass before they realise they have been at it for a long time.

Employees that show inspiration in their work are typically the ones who have bravely moved around and tried different jobs and organisations until finding a role where they are very happy, feel needed and feel like they are using their talents for the greater good of the organisation.

Examples abound of passionate employees but this one stands above others in my mind.

Tony the HP Printer Cartridge salesman was an Italian American and Yankees fan from New York City. Tony and I were both asked to speak at HP's Asian Sales Conference in Singapore. When Tony was asked about the environmental friendliness of the ink in the printer cartridges, he proceeded to break open a cartridge and eat the black powder right in front of the room. The audience, in shock, was rapt with attention as Tony, black indelible ink powder dropping from his mouth, proceeded to tell the audience the ink was not only environmentally friendly it was even good enough to eat. To this day, everyone in the ballroom at the Grand Hyatt will remember Tony's passion for his job and how he inspired everyone he worked with. It is not surprising that Tony was one of HP's top salesmen in the world at that time and that is why he was flown to Singapore to share his knowledge and experience.

Tony's story is not only one of personal passion. Successful organisations also need to know the passions of their employees and put them into jobs where they will realise their potential. This talent management is obviously easier in larger organisations that feature a greater variety and availability of jobs. Many of the best employers in the world today avail themselves of assessment tools to identify people's passions, strengths and competencies and they seriously explore ways to move their people into roles best suited to their strengths. HP did just that with Tony.

One of my clients asked me to dialogue with his son Sam to help uncover what career Sam might best choose for his career. Sam was at the point of entry exams for university. Through dialogue and assessment, it was clear that his interests were focused on legal work but in his head, he wanted to be an investment banker. Investment banking is attractive to many people who want to make the millions of dollars common to bankers today but the job itself is not for everyone. One of the most important decisions you will need to assess is whether you want to save the world or fill your bank account. I did not believe Sam would excel as an investment banker because his interest in results were second to his interest in rationale.

Most people do not have access to assessments or talent management and so in your own career development it is important that you invest in learning more about yourself. I recommend the *Strength Deployment Inventory* (Scudder) from Personal Strengths Publishing (where I have been a master trainer for a long time) or *MBTI* (Myers-Briggs), I qualified with Psychometrics Canada for work with Disney, or *Strengths Finder* (Buckingham) from Gallop Corporation (I linked their findings with my work for Standard Chartered Bank). In the old days, people measured strengths and trained weaknesses.   Today smart organisations measure strengths and move people to leverage their strengths realising you achieve far greater results getting people to do what they love and love what they do than training them to do things they don't necessarily like or excel at.

"As Richard Logan found in his study of individuals who survived severe physical ordeals
– polar explorers wandering alone in the Arctic, concentration camp inmates –
one common attitude shared by such people
was the implicit belief that their destiny was in their hands.
They did not doubt their own resources would be sufficient
to allow them to determine their fate." (Csikszentmihalyi)

Organisation

Another aspect of inspiration is ensuring the mission of your organisation or community is inherently motivating to your team. I have had great fun working with Disney employees who remember the magic Pixie Dust which they themselves experienced as children and enjoy sharing that same magic with children today. Employees that I have worked with at Expedia and Google are passionate about how their technologies are revolutionising entire industries. Staff at orphanages across Asia who are bringing happiness to abandoned children, or teachers that revel in seeing their students learn or doctors many of whom studied medicine because someone they knew personally suffered the effects of an illness they are now working to counteract.

I worked with Johnson Electric, one of the world's largest micro motor manufacturers. Their mission is to sell micro motors to all companies that use them such as consumer products manufacturers e.g. hairdryers; motor vehicle manufacturers e.g. window wipers, power tools e.g. drills etc. To accommodate sales growth the company decided to split into several divisions, each one focusing on a specific customer market. In this case the mission dictated the organisation chart.

In Europe I audited Phillip Morris, the world's largest cigarette manufacturer at the time. Their mission was to diversify the group to protect shareholder wealth while accommodating the world's dropping cigarette sales in response to health concerns. While their unstated mission had evolved from being the world's #1 cigarette manufacturer to being the protector of shareholder wealth, one decision may be to stop manufacturing cigarettes. When I asked the person responsible for countering the anti-smoking campaigns around the world how he lived with himself given what is now known about the ill-effects of smoking his response was simply to say "it's a job". When people are inspired and, on a mission, they do not accept compromising situations by simply describing it as a job.

It was reported that GSK was fined in China for inappropriate activities resulting in the jailing in China of one of their consultants. After this embarrassing event and the fines which came with it, GSK reviewed its mission and now presumably do not act questionably when looking to expand market share. The opposite is true for ISIS which is clearly doing questionable things to attract young people to join their jihad. ISIS is on the run and might not last forever but it can be argued that is has been an influential group despite the terrible activities that it espouses. People working for ISIS are so inspired they are prepared to surrender their lives.

One client I worked with did not surrender his life for his beliefs but he did surrender a 7-digit salary. Soon after getting promoted to the highest level of his professional firm Jim decided to resign (he was too young to retire) and move to Europe to do something completely different. Jim's inspiration came from the work, the career ladder and juggling the work inherent with his senior position. It became clear however that soon after he had "arrived" (as others aiming for similar promotions would call it), Jim decided to quit because his mission and inspiration had been achieved. Now Jim is living in Europe and playing with his grandchildren.

At the national level I look at the inspiration of the Koreans who donated their own jewellery to help the nation out of debt following the currency crisis of 1998. Not only was Korea the first country to exit IMF support, I even attended a Korean Pop concert in Hong Kong where Koreans collectively celebrated the tearing up of their national debt. I cannot imagine Canadians sending their gold to Ottawa in hope of erasing the national debt.

It is also easy to see the lack of inspiration in people, organisations, and communities. Today many people are worried about the growing number of young people who spend most of their waking hours glued to the computer while expressing boredom and adding to the ranks of suicide and substance abuse. People who are inspired and aligned in their mission, whatever that may be, are not the ones wasting their lives on-line, on drugs or self-harming. This is not only an issue of youth because a lot of employees are bored, unmotivated, and under-utilised at work these days.

When asked to help with the merger of Exxon and Mobil I met a petrol-chemical engineer in Malaysia who argued against the change management training the company was running to facilitate the integration of their two giant work forces in Asia. He was having nothing of it. When I asked what he was passionate about he told me he was retiring and that it was to be the biggest change in his life. Instead of focusing on work I suggested he focus the day applying the change management techniques to his transition into retirement. At the start of the day he was ready to walk out but by the end of the day, as he looked up at the Petronas Twin Towers shining in the setting sun across the park from our meeting venue, he told me, "this has been the most valuable day he has spent in years".

The secret is to tap into people's passions, find out what they are and spend time talking about these so as employers we can find ways to incorporate people's passions into their work. I have worked with organisations where the people are clearly bored and boring. These tend to be middle managers who don't feel any autonomy over their work, find themselves doing jobs they don't particularly enjoy and refuse to change because they don't see a natural next step and lack the bravery to step into the unknown. In some markets these are also the same people that go on strike because for them it is not the work that inspires them it is the pay and perks that come along with the job. You never see inspired people go on strike, instead it is always the ones who have grown alienated from their work/employers and are simply interested in WIIFM (what is in it for me).

One inspired organisation I work with is UNICEF. It is fun to work with UNICEF professionals because they are inspired to save the children of the world and every time there is a crisis these people become even more important and inspiring.

"The best moments usually occur when a person's body or mind is stretched to its limits in a voluntary effort to accomplish something difficult and worthwhile." (Csikszentmihalyi)

National

At the national level, we also see people lack inspiration. Just think about bureaucrats that live a faceless life behind the glass of their government departments without a care about the taxpayers desire for fast and efficient service. People who have lived under repressive regimes understand the excitement of 1989 when the wall crumbled in Eastern Europe and people fled joyously into a brave new world. Governments that do not create the environments for their people to find and realise their passions will instead watch as their talent migrates to better markets such as they are doing today in greater numbers than ever before.

The world's recurring protests are driven by people who in their passion to protest are demonstrating their unhappiness with the stifling nature of the economies or governance regimes in which they live. Typically, in these situations few if any of the leaders "inside the walls of affluence" venture out to dialogue with to the people and help them realise their dreams.

When the students of Hong Kong protested in the 2014 Umbrella Movement the passion and inspiration on the streets was palpable. On several occasions I spent the whole night with the students talking to them about their dreams, ambitions, fears, and inexperience fuelling their movement. Just like the French Revolution inspired a generation of activists, so too did the Umbrella Movement with romance and fierce intellectual debates taking place in the tent communities stretched out on the main highway bisecting Hong Kong.

At the same time the students were protesting in the streets, I was working with a variety of Hong Kong government departments. The absence of inspiration in the corridors of power was astonishing and public servants said the problem was the students. These government employees failed to look at themselves in the mirror, content to continue collecting their pay while overseeing the longest drawn out people protest in a major city anywhere in the world. Part of the problem in Hong Kong is that the Government has lost its mission.

The 2019 democracy protests also showed incredible inspiration by those directly involved and even those on the side-lines that would come out for example in the two-million-person march in the summer of 2019. As protests morphed into destruction and destruction morphed into China's national security law, inspired words are heard from all corners of this debate. Success however has stumbled at dialogue and openness, two more hurdles discussed later in this book.

The students of Hong Kong reminded me of the students I taught in Mainland China in the early 1990's many of whom had been in Tiananmen Square in the days and weeks leading up to the June 4th incident (as Beijing refers to their military slaughter of hundreds of students). My students were inspired by their national leaders talk of change and by the opening of the Soviet Union. Their passion for positive change, like young people everywhere, is what brought them into the city squares by the tens of thousands. After the military crackdown and the brutal suppression of dreams all the students I spoke to about this had survivor guilt and had shifted their focus to getting rich and getting out of China as soon as possible. Many have done exactly that.

The political inspiration I found in Burma (Myanmar) was also palpable. On my first visit leader Aung San Suu Kyi was under house arrest. I was told not to visit the country because I would enrich the military junta by visiting. I went to witness the situation and report back. Once in Rangoon I was told not to visit the national leader's house but I went anyway, my taxi driver happy to show me her lake front home. Finally, I was told not to take photos so I rolled down my window and took photos of the large fence cutting off the street from the front lawn of the house. When I visited, "the lady" had been under house arrest for 18 years.

The second time I visited Burma was in 2015 just after the election won by Aung San Suu Kyi. People everywhere were jubilant that she had won but time will tell whether she is able make change happen. The Lady inspires a good portion of her country's population but her international reputation was hurt by her government's failure to protect the Rohingya people who have lived for many generations and yet remained stateless inside Myanmar. The success of the Buddhists in Myanmar cannot be attained at the expense of the Muslim Rohingya. My discussion on Potentialism addresses this reality. The 21st century is one of diversity amongst people.

Inspiration is also driven by passions at a national level. Countries like Thailand, famous for their welcoming culture, are well suited to host the millions of tourists which visit every year. Hong Kong on the other hand, known for their passion for results, had to learn how to serve customers lovingly at HK Disneyland (they are still learning). Germany, famous for their engineering led manufacturing culture, bring their rational style to everything they do including for example the introduction of robotics into manufacturing.

Although Hong Kongers want to excel personally and do well in this regard, the city itself, once considered Asia's World City, lost its way when it became just another Chinese city. Since the return of Hong Kong to the Mainland, many believe its main competitor - Singapore, has done a much better job attracting talent and improving its infrastructure.

I lived through the inspired nationalism of French Canada from the terrorism of 1970 to the election of the separatist government in Quebec in 1976. Through the nearly 50 years of nationalistic separatism in Quebec I met people so inspired by the idea they were willing to kill the economy they worked in to achieve their goal. In 1978 I joined a small group of friends and travelled to Sherbrooke to see the charismatic separatist leader Rene Levesque speak to his jubilant crowd of thousands at the local arena. Nationalism and anti-English sentiment was everywhere which meant I dressed to look French and I kept my mouth shut for fear of my accent revealing my English identity. In that era, it was common for English speakers to be beat up if they ventured into separatist areas.

At the same time, I met people so opposed to the ideas of the separatists they literally wanted to "shoot the bastards" and eventually one did. When inspiration turns to extremism everyone loses and this was the case of Quebec where the economy suffered terribly and the separatists never achieved their goal. Now fifty years later young people in Quebec question the inspiration of their parents and grand-parents during that era and are themselves more interested in getting jobs and getting ahead in the global world of the 21st century.

A final example is that of Bunker Roy, founder of Barefoot College, an international NGO responsible for improving living standards for the poor by teaching women how to set up and operate solar panels to provide electricity in villages not previously connected to the grid. This enables the villagers to do things such as pump water from wells, study after dark and use computers connected to the internet. People who have met Bunker Roy are impressed most by his inspiration which is infectious and which borders on anger with people who do not want to help. This unflagging passion to change the world has led to improved living standards for millions of people. For this and for his inspiration Time Magazine named Bunker Roy one of the world's 100 most influential people.

Solutions

So, what to do when you do not know your calling or mission? At the personal level I recommend doing a lot of different jobs. Gain experience, volunteer, push out your comfort zone and ask your employers, family, friends and co-workers for feedback to better understand what you like, what you don't like, where you excel and where you fall behind others. I believe we all have our niche and that it is our duty to realise our potential while helping others realise theirs. Assessment tools like the SDI or 360-degree feedback are also a great way to learn about yourself in your quest to realise your potential.

It is also important to realise that things change and that what you do early in your career is not necessarily where you will excel later in your career. Some leave behind their technical careers to become managers of others doing the same thing e.g. teachers that become principals or lawyers that become partners. Some people specialise in a niche area of their industry realising they may have a strength in a technical area or through their vast network of relationships they specialise in business development. Some people eventually change directions and build into a new area that is open to them. Saving your money, recognising your competencies, managing your network of contacts, and keeping your eyes and ears open for opportunities are all important if you are to enjoy successful careers over the 40-60 years of your working lives.

At the organisational and national levels, it is important to give your employees training, development and talent management but it is equally important to ensure alignment with the company vision and mission and to address slippage in alignment as things change (which they always do). Don't allow "lack of budget" to be an excuse for not getting together periodically with your teams to assess what has changed and review *what* you are doing, *how* you are doing it and *why* you are doing it to identify and correct misalignment.

I helped an Indonesian conglomerate identify their misalignment and begin to negotiate change when it became apparent that their very profitable push into palm oil was at juxtapositions with their ideal of being environmentally friendly. Of course, it is not always easy to address ambiguity but it is important to recognise the best results are achieved by people "whistling on the way to work" not fighting over what they are doing. In this regard both inspiration and lack of inspiration can fuel the courage and bravery you need to make a change because without it little if anything will work in your favour. Successful people, organisations and nations are inspired.

In summary:

1. At the personal level, it is important to do as many different jobs as possible so you can identify what you like and do not like. It is also useful to acquire feedback on your preferences by asking people around you and completing psychometric assessments such as the SDI by Core Strengths (let me know if you are interested).

2. In organisations, you want to ensure feedback mechanisms are in place and enable people to work in tasks where they show competence and interest.

3. At the national level, it is important to help people learn their passions, to create opportunities for individuals and organisations to achieve their potential and to pay attention to all the people, organisations, and countries left behind because they will soon find their way to your doorstep asking for help.

Sustainable

Short term	Honest
Corrupt	Future Focus
Self focus	Transparent

"Sumoud, an Arabic word meaning
steadfastness, endurance, and perseverance in the face of adversity
– all passive traits lacking in glamour." (Shehadeh)

Individual

A noticeable trait of long-established leaders, organisations and nations is that most of their investment is focused on sustainable value creation. Leaders invest their time in activities and ideas that enhance their future. Companies develop systems and people that add to their bottom line. Nations build societal values with commensurate social services that can last generations into the future. It is also easy to identify people, organisations and nations doing the exact opposite. Through some misconceived view of the future leaders focus on short-term pleasures, companies rip out savings to pay their executives or invest in ill-conceived or biased investments and nations literally poor concrete (and tax dollars) into the ground building such things as Olympic installations and military armaments that are used once.

At a personal level leader that focus on the future and demonstrate transparent, honest integrity are the ones we turn to with our hopes in leading us into the future. These leaders have personal needs as well but have learned to manage their own desires enabling them to help others in need. As my Uncle George Ewing used to say, "you can't manage others until you can manage yourself". He was mayor of Melbourne, Quebec, and founder of a successful furniture business which operated there until he retired.

The longer you spend leading the more experience you have encountering situations where corruption or self-interest detracts from sustainability and which force you to reconsider your own position. At these points, you need to decide between what you consider as right and wrong and proceed bravely into the unknown.

Organisations

One finance director I know challenged a transaction pointing out what the managing director wanted to do was in fact against generally accepted accounting principles and as such this finance director would never authorize it. This decision (bravely taken and inspired by knowing what is right and wrong in terms of accounting) led to the firing of the finance director. Once a new finance director was hired the managing director forced through the transaction (to the detriment of the shareholders and the company). Such situations happen day in and day out. As leaders, we need to know for ourselves how we will decide between right and wrong, yes, and no, when difficult situations present themselves as grey rather than as black and white.

Another director of finance that I worked with (in Geneva) showed his solid integrity when he blew the whistle on the corruption at WorldCom. His actions in the local subsidiary eventually led to the collapse of the company and $US3.8 billion in losses. Smartly he recognized that the expenses he was being asked to authorize were unsustainable and signing off on unsubstantiated transactions would not pass his desk. His actions not only resulted in one of the biggest bankruptcies in history, it also led to the US enacting the Sarbanes-Oxley Act, the most sweeping business regulations since the depression.

One of the good management books of recent times is by Simon Sinek (Start with Why). Sinek reminds us that it is not so much what we do or how we do it but rather why we do what we do that enables people to assess, help or forget us. For example, what I do is help people achieve improved outcomes through dialogue and negotiation. How I do this is through writing, speaking, training, and consulting. What attracts people is why I do it and for me the reason I do what I do is because I believe we have a duty to realise our potential while helping others realise theirs (see chapter on Potentialism). It is as simple as that. The best outcome is not what is best for me but what is best for you and me.

Leaders that want sustainability should think of themselves in a long distance run rather than a short sprint to the finish line. Take your time; plan; focus on the right things; do not get distracted; remain focused. All these things help achieve personal sustainable success. Unfortunately, there are endless examples of leaders losing focus of the long term and taking decisions that at best are ill informed and at worst corrupt. Money managers treat people badly favouring financial results instead, pharmaceutical managers calculate liability versus doing the right thing and people knowingly steal from others. All these people are investing in short term unsustainable outcomes.

Effective leaders which invest in sustainable projects may see the fruit of their labour eventually fall and stumble. I think here of my father who dedicated his life to sustainable trusteeship only to see everything he ever worked on eventually ended. The companies he worked for were merged and eventually closed. The hospital he ran was closed. The clubs he was a member of and the schools he attended all closed. We are reminded that everything changes in time but if we are on our watch we should be focused on sustainable futures and then, as it says in the locker room of the Montreal Canadiens ice hockey team, one of the most successful sports franchises in history:

To you from failing hands we throw
The torch; be yours to hold it high. (McRae)

The world's leading accounting firms and leading brands in other industries have practices less successful competitors do not. These leading companies use their better margins to afford global best practices, use internal controls, professional advice, invest in training and development, manage their talent effectively and make smart investments. This allows them to both produce at lower costs while at the same time invest in new technologies and divest of sunset service lines.

Companies that renew themselves and stay at the top of their game over generations require all the attributes described here but especially bravery and openness to remain sustainable over time. A good example was IBM's sale of its laptop business which at the time seemed crazy but people knowledgeable understood the rapid evolution to hand-held devices and the diminishing market for laptops. The sale of the company to Lenovo was good for both parties because although laptops were a sunset industry globally there were still hundreds of millions of PC's to be sold in China where Lenovo was based. When assessing your sustainability, you also need to consider opportunity cost. IBM realized that they could sell their personal computer division and use the capital to invest in better ROE elsewhere to maintain their edge in other parts of the computer market.

One of my clients sent their entire legal division to attend an industry conference where they learned that making small changes to their current policies and procedures would give them a slight advantage over the competition. Since the leaders attended the conference together and agreed on the changes required, the changes were affected immediately. Sustainability is as much to do about multiple small decisions as it is about big decisions (like IBM).

Sometimes decision making does not go well, and sustainability is not the goal even though they say it is. Family businesses will often stay too long in sunset industries and other investments for the simple reason they have always been there. One multi-national I worked with took a global decision to cut back their Asian investment and focus on Europe and North America even though Asia was showing the fastest growth in the whole company. Why did they cut off their foot to save the leg? Europe and North America held sway on the board and basically out-voted Asia to protect their personal interests. This personal vs corporate interest trade-off is common hence the importance of my earlier remarks on a leader's personal sustainability.

Another business owner I worked for engaged me to build the "sense of ownership" of their employees. When I asked the majority shareholder of this listed conglomerate if he was offering them shares or options he laughed and said, "of course not". "So, you want them to have a sense of ownership but not actually be owners", I asked incredulously. Most of those employees have now left the organization while the owner is still there. One-way companies can enhance their sustainability is to share ownership with key employees they want to lock into the future of the business. Without competitive incentives (one of my old bosses told me in Canada) "the good people leave, and the mediocre people move up" leaving average people in charge.

Market forces are a great teacher. One of my consumer product clients in Hong Kong decided to improve the sustainability of their HR department by making them into a profit centre. Headquarters believed this decision would help prune the less effective employees and force an end to practices no longer considered core to the company strategy. To everyone's surprise however none of the group companies bought the services of the HR department preferring to handle these functions themselves. The result was the closure of the HR department in only six months and everyone getting fired. Sometimes sustainability requires significant change. One client I know gave only three days' notice to all employees before closing the business. The goal of this shareholder was sustainability of the holding company not the investee business.

All the best companies that I have worked with have created world class leadership development programmes to create a sustainable supply of future leadership for their organisations. After helping build the award winning programme at Coopers & Lybrand in the early 90's I then went on to help design and deliver similarly successful leadership and talent development programmes for Disney, Marriott, the Malaysian Government and many more.

Sustainable organisations also have clearly defined career development paths that enable them to recruit the best university graduates and keep building their careers over years. The large accounting firms have clear development programmes increasing authority, responsibility, training, and performance feedback annually as promotions continue until they become leaders of the firm. Performance management systems are an important part of ensuring the sustainability of the system because people should not be promoted until they are ready and corrective actions are needed to help those not yet (or ever) suitable for promotion. Corrective action might include coaching, training, moving people sideways or out of the organization. In my situation, I chose lateral moves to gain international and training experience before climbing to the point where I chose to set up my own business. Companies interested in sustainability need to work hard to keep their talent because it takes at least a decade to develop these people and losing them after this investment is very costly.

Some companies are dropping the annual performance appraisal system finding them poorly adopted and unpopular. Instead these organisations are relying on effective feedback during the work cycle and not waiting until year-end to have this conversation.

Sustainable organisations also need to keep an eye on technological change. I used to write for my college newspaper and would type my copy on my Smith Corona typewriter. Smith Corona had a significant share of the keyboard market but completely missed the advent of computers that within a few short years had wiped out the typewriter market which had existed for over a hundred of years.

Sustainable organisations must also ensure they are fiscally responsible. When the professors of one of my favourite universities voted themselves, a pension increase they disregarded the ballooning pension plan deficit which, like a national deficit or overrun on your credit card, means that after nearly 200 years of history the university could go bankrupt if it had to pay out 100% of its pension liabilities today.

National

At the community and national levels, it is the values that are sustainable. Institutions come and go based on what is required to sustain the values. Tibetan culture has sustained itself for thousands of years but the way this has been done has changed significantly over the last one hundred years. American values are similar despite the appearance of chaos in the USA now. The same can be said of religions and international charities all of which have long outlived their founders.

Some communities and nations are not practicing sustainable behaviours. Wherever you see excessive pollution, high cost of living or civil strife you know people will not be living profitably in those places long into the future. Likewise, people want freedom of thought and expression and innovative environments in which to flourish. Silicon Valley will continue to excel sustainably into the future because of the underlying values which attract people from around the world to give their ideas, energy and waking hours while in return gaining satisfaction, fun, friendships, and financial reward. While people eventually move on and die, successful underlying values live on if the local population continues.

The crack down on the Arab Spring was a pre-cursor to the mass migration towards Europe. Quebec's crackdown on language of business was a precursor to the mass migration to Toronto, Vancouver and beyond. Nations that want to thrive into the future must focus on retaining and developing their talent. Anything less is unsustainable and will leave governments with old people to look after but without young people to pay the taxes.

In July 1989 I stood looking East to no man's land from West Berlin saying to my local hotel manager that soon his hotel would be worth a lot of money since it stood right smack in the middle of the future unified city. He however was too close to the situation to see how quickly the political situation was changing. I had arrived with my wife in West Berlin from the other side of the Iron Curtain passing through Czechoslovakia, Hungary, East Germany, and East Berlin before crossing at Checkpoint Charlie to arrive into West Berlin. My hotel manager thought back to the decades of lost hope and lives since the wall went up during the height of the Cold War. Fortunately, he was wrong, and the wall came down within months. East Germany collapsed and Berlin and Germany were unified for the first time since WW2. Populations are sustainable but political regimes are not unless they serve rather than control their populations.

I returned to Berlin in 1999, ten years after the collapse of the wall and was intrigued to visit sites in the Eastern half of the city that were opened to tourists. Sites included underground bunkers used by the Nazi's and rooftop bars catering to the new creative talent flooding into the city. What was also noticeable was the enduring dislike between West Germans whose taxes were still paying for East Germans finding it impossible to fit into the modern economy and jobs of the new Germany. Back in 1989 the difference between East and West caused us to feel like we were jumping back 30+ years as we crossed through Checkpoint Charlie separating the two sides of the city. By 1999 the differences were less visible but the cultural behaviour of the East Germans had little changed.

In the national arena, nothing is forever. Although we aim for sustainability, we should also recognize that borders are man-made and change over time. It was a unique opportunity to see the fall of the wall in Eastern Europe in 1989 but it was also historic to witness firsthand the handover of Hong Kong from Britain to China in 1997. The lease for Hong Kong's New Territories had ended and realizing it was impossible to sustain Hong Kong Island and the bit of Kowloon up to Boundary Street which Britain owned in perpetuity, then Prime Minister Margaret Thatcher signed away the future of Hong Kong to China's then paramount leader Deng Xiao Peng. The lease expired at midnight on June 30th, 1997. In the week leading up to the handover (or the "take back" as it was referred to in China) I was in Beijing meeting Mainland Chinese jubilantly photograph the "take back" clock which counted down the years, months, days, minutes, and seconds to midnight June 30th.

The mood in Hong Kong leading up to the handover was considerably different. On the evening of June 30th, I had declined the invitation to work (as VIP host) inside the Hong Kong Convention and Exhibition Centre where hundreds of world leaders would witness the handover in person. Instead my wife Marie and I joined friends on a converted DB Ferry in the harbour where we joined other boats marking the occasion. On our launch, we enjoyed champagne and bagpipes then returned to the DB Resident's Club before midnight to watch the ceremony eating roast beef and Yorkshire pudding. The celebratory mood of the mainlanders in Tiananmen Square was juxtaposed to that of the Hong Kong Chinese whose sadness and tears witnessed in the club that evening showed the depression and worry they felt over their future. In the lead-up to handover Hong Kong Chinese were emigrating by the tens of thousands to Canada, Australia, the UK, and many other countries, fearing for the safety of their lives and savings under the rule of China's Communist Party. Local newspapers included advertisements and advise for obtaining passports from countries all over the world.

In the generation since handover Hong Kong has flourished but now things seem to be changing again and for the first-time locals are talking about separating from China to become an independent nation like Singapore. Whatever the outcome, the important thing is for the government leaders in both Hong Kong and Beijing to design a sustainable future for the people of Hong Kong because if they don't talent with the option to emigrate will do so leaving behind an aging society costing Beijing more than they wish to afford. Since the imposition of the national security law the only thing that has changed is that people are no longer allowed to talk about independence, but many still think about it. As you will read however in the chapter on the importance of partnership, the future is about working together and helping each other realise their potential, not imposing your will by force on another.

In terms of sustainability I was aiming to influence Iran's leadership when I explained that their national interests would be better served if their President at the time stopped saying Israel should be wiped off the face of the earth. Iran and Israel need to be reminded that we must all learn to live together on this little planet otherwise we are all at risk.

Sustainable governments must also realise they are not overseeing a zero-sum game whereby helping one group means ignoring another group. In the province of Quebec, the French speaking government has created endless policy in the last fifty years to benefit the French speaking population at the detriment of the English population. Thus, the English population and investment has dwindled to the detriment of the French population. Better are policies that support one group without hindering another. Economist John Nash won the Nobel prize proving in his Governing Dynamics that optimal outcomes are achieved not when you help yourself but when you help both yourself and the other stakeholders. Nash's Equilibrium Point is the point at which one party cannot achieve more without costing another party something. In Quebec, English businesses, schools, universities, and hospitals can all grow without forcing a detrimental impact upon their French counterparts. In other words, it is possible to grow the pie before splitting the pie, so everyone benefits. Society is not a zero-sum game.

I am asked to serve the 1% and happily do so because these people and their companies have the resources to invest in the best solutions globally. By working with this group, I share my best practices and at the same time I learn from them and take my learning to help the remaining 99%. My Robin Hood approach of gaining fees and experience from wealthy companies to help less profitable organisations and NGO's is not new, and it is sustainable. What is not sustainable is the growing divergence between the rich and poor called the Gini Index. As we have seen through history, once the gap between the rich and poor gets too wide people revolt, violence redistributes wealth and the gap narrows again.

Another unsustainable situation is the corruption I have witnessed in the harvesting of forests and oceans. In Malaysia and Indonesia, the slash and burn of natural forests followed by the planting of monoculture Palm Oil is profitable in the short term but damaging overall to the wildlife that lose their habitat and the environment that benefits from diverse forests to prevent flooding, replenish soil nutrients etc. In terms of the sustainability of oceans one only needs walk the wet markets of Asia to see the wholesale rape and pillage of fish and seafood. Many species of fish are now collapsing as they are unable to sustain their populations in the face of the unrelenting harvesting taking place offshore and out of view of national governments which in many cases are paid off to look the other way.

We need to use our scientific knowledge to change the laws that regulate our behavior. When as a teenager, I worked at the Tamaracouta Scout Reserve (the longest running scout camp in the world) it quickly became obvious we could no longer build latrines and harvest fire wood if we wanted the lands and forests of the Reserve to be sustainable. Instead we forced change and now campers use environmentally friendly toilets and natural gas instead of firewood (still not carbon neutral but better than before). The camp itself is now searching for a new way to remain sustainable in this new era where youth prefer activities other than scouting and camping in the outdoors, a valuable reminder that sustainability means remaining alert to changes of all kinds.

Sometimes our efforts to protect the environment are prevented from happening. This was experienced in Samut Prakarn Thailand when the Asian Development Bank installed a wastewater treatment plant to treat pollutants streaming from factories into the Chao Praya River. Local villagers believed the wastewater treatment plant would damage their shrimp beds and revolted against the construction threatening the lives of the engineers building the plant. Science is important but so too is the ability to convince local people to change their ways especially given that sometimes local people are illiterate and often less educated and culturally threatened by outsiders forcing change they did not request. When science is debatable the solution is in the dialogue.

Solutions

To build sustainability at the personal, corporate, and national levels I offer three key concepts.

1. When I was an accountant, I learned that my main job was not to do the accounts it was to produce more accountants. If we are to build sustainable futures, we need to develop people to take over from us so we can move onto new things. When China was developing rapidly in the 1990's they needed 1 million accountants. I was busy training groups of 20-40 at a time but at that rate it would take over 10,000 years.

2. If the world is to get ahead, we ALL must get involved in helping develop others. As I like to put it, we have a duty to realise our potential while helping others realise theirs (Potentialism).

3. One of the best models I have found for development is called *Situational Leadership* by Hersey and Blanchard. The concept is straightforward and involves telling people what to do (and how to do it), coaching them as they gain skill, experience, and confidence, and then, only when they are ready, delegate to them and move onto other things yourself.

Trusteeship

Selfish	Builder
Uncaring	Protectors
Egotistical	Legacy

"The results –
like the growing gap between rich and poor and the ongoing assault on earth's vitality
– strongly suggest that business needs new ways of thinking.
"It's not short versus long term," the Dalai Lama points out. "We need both.
But there's too much obsessive focus on the short term
regardless of long-term consequences." (Goleman)

Individual

I define Trusteeship as leaders managing resources and relationships in a way that protects and enhances their value for future generations. Such behavior seemed to be a lot more important in my childhood in Canada than it is today in my adulthood in Asia. Perhaps this is because Canada is a young country populated by peoples that emigrated from other countries with only the pack on their back and progressively built the institutions Canadian society enjoys today. Perhaps the difference results from the incredible wealth gap that has emerged creating the illusion of endless wealth which has permitted some people to discard things of the past and purchase anew. Perhaps it is because technological change and evolution in materials science has suggested that valuable things passed down generation after generation (e.g. books, furniture, tools etc.) are now "old" and should be discarded or given away in favour of new items more closely suited to current needs. Perhaps it is because corporate earnings have ballooned providing some people with excessive wealth and giving them the option of discarding assets hard fought by previous generations.

It is not only personal heirlooms that are being discarded today, so too are our institutions and even our norms all of which are struggling to survive the onslaught of globalization and change. We must not confuse keeping things as they were with reinforcing the underlying values while moving with the times. A few examples will help you understand what I am referring to.

My great grandfather, Dr. AR Griffith, was one of the founders of the Montreal Homeopathic Hospital. At the time of its formation in 1894 it stood on Montreal's prestigious Sherbrooke Street corner McGill College avenue facing Canada's leading McGill University's. My great grandfather lived just a few blocks away on Peel Street inside Montreal's Golden Square Mile which at the time housed over 80% of Canada' wealth.

The underlying values of that era involved bringing world best practices in medicine and homeopathy (the two were regarded equally then) to the bustling community in need. Wealthy families paid more, poor families paid what they could or nothing at all and doctors, led by their Hippocratic Oath, did what they could to serve whoever arrived at their doors.

In time the hospital's reputation and the growth of the community meant that a bigger location was needed so in 1927 the Hospital moved several blocks west to a new building cornering Sherbrooke Street and Marlowe Avenue. In 1951 the hospital was renamed the Queen Elizabeth Hospital in honour of the then wife of King George VI, and who was soon to become the Queen Mother of Britain's current Queen Elizabeth II.

My great grandfather was a strict Baptist and obviously a stern enforcer of a good education and living a "Christian" life. My mother spoke of no sports on Sundays which must have been tough for her at the time since she eventually became a physical education teacher.

The unstated Griffith family values of **service, sacrifice and excellence** meant the hospital was the home of many firsts. As outlined in the book *Who Killed the Queen*, in the 100-year history of this little institution it became known the world over for such things as:
1. Outstanding treatment of nurses, uncommon in that era
2. The first use of curare in clinical anaesthesia, a breakthrough for which Harold Griffith (Dr.' AR's son) became famous - there remains to this day Griffith lectures around the world and a permanent chair in his name at McGill University
3. The first Chinese woman doctor hired in Canada (1949)
4. The first ICU in Canada
5. First use of preoperative antibiotics
6. Considered the best primary and secondary teaching hospital in Canada
7. Considered the best community hospital in Canada
8. The most efficient hospital with the fastest operating theatre changeover time of any hospital in Canada
9. First accredited mammography service in Canada
10. Early adoption and leading work in X-Ray technology, ENT, laparoscopy, and laser surgery

In 1961, the year I was born, the hospital was renovated and reopened by the then Premier of Quebec, Jean Lesage who called it "Canada's largest little hospital" but by 1995, with Canada reeling in debt the hospital was closed by the provincial government. Some say the British name of the hospital riled the separatist government of the day which had also lost its separatist referendum by just over 1% (a margin smaller than the number of spoiled votes) that same year. The hospital closed, the assets were sold and its much-loved teaching hospital link to McGill University, which had been so valuable for so long, was ended.

After the institution closed the community joined forces and took matters into their own hands to create a new entity and continue the tradition of healthcare delivery in the premises of this once world-famous hospital. Today it is a not-for-profit health organization with no government funding just like it was when Dr AR first opened its doors in 1894.

The founders and subsequent leaders of this organisation kept it going as effective trustees through the First World War, the great depression, the second world war, the nationalisation of healthcare and the exodus of the English from Quebec. During its lifetime, the hospital was run by a family member for most of its existence including my great-grandfather, his sons and then my father. It was only a few short years after direct family ties had come to an end that the hospital closed. The trusteeship of leaders focused on the long-term preservation and success of the institution is what allowed it to survive the traumas of history, profit from the good times and save for the bad. Once this mentality was lost people took more than needed from the budget and not surprisingly the end was nigh.

Trusteeship involves strategic leadership, good fiscal management, lifelong learning, and effective investment. Service, sacrifice, and excellence - the same underlying behaviours which made the hospital successful brought success to other parts of Montreal society in that gilded era including business, science, technology, education, sports, and leisure.

Trusteeship reminds us things last longer if maintained but Buddhist philosophy reminds us that change is inevitable and therefore the only things that can remain are the underlying values such as service, sacrifice, and excellence.

The forces against trusteeship are many but none is worse than personal greed which shows itself in corruption, materialism, and bias for one group over another. Individuals bent on personal gain in today's world benefit themselves in the short term to the detriment of the greater good in the long term. The effect is like people turning up their air conditioners on a hot day to cool off when in fact if we all do this the earth warms and we all lose. The fact the world's economic divide is worse than it has ever been has a lot to do with the loss of trusteeship in popular culture. In Drew Dillinger's poem (see below) the shamanic prayer the dreamer's distant descendants ask when you could act, why did you do nothing? The prayer could be extended by having distant descendants ask, "why did you take more than needed and leave us with nothing?"

School curriculums today are doing a good job teaching young people about the importance of social and environmental trusteeship. Youth enjoying a gap year often travel to parts of the world where they can offer service to those in need. Some parts of the world are building a generation much better focused on the collective good rather than personal gain. Similarly NGO's like Leaders Quest are helping leaders grapple with their choices both personally and in their senior roles in the private and public sector. By helping leaders gain first-hand experience with all stakeholder groups in tough situations (e.g. Israel and Palestine) NGO's are helping improve decision making and the values of trusteeship which arise from understanding we all live together on our finite planet.

Organisations

Some examples that spring to mind of lack of trusteeship in organisations today include professors of a small university that voted themselves pension increases when they knew the unfunded pension liabilities they were creating could in time bankrupt the several hundred year old institution.

Another example of a lack of trusteeship is one of my resource extraction clients where employees in a different division of the company asked why the company was destroying their country's environment simply for exports to foreigners.

Another situation saw employees of a significant telecom license operator negotiate losses for their employer on the basis that they would receive bonuses for deals struck even in situations where the deals themselves were bad for the company overall.

And of course, the worst of all is corruption which takes many forms but is best described as theft. On several occasions, I have witnessed large financial institutions stand by their large corporate clients at the expense of their small clients or suppliers after having calculated the cost of loss in financial rather than reputational terms.

Trusteeship in organisations today is commonly called Corporate Governance or Corporate Social Responsibility (CSR) and is sometimes measured in economic terms by assets under management or triple bottom line (profit, social and environment). One organisation I have been honoured to work with, UNICEF, has developed "the blue book" of corporate governance best practices to ensure the donations received in Hong Kong are managed as effectively as possible and passed onto those most in need.

Trusteeship is not always so easy but compassion will often tell you which way to go. In helping a Canadian business owner sort out the governance of his small but profitable business it became clear that his father-in-law was costing the company a lot of money without any commensurate value in return. Wanting to manage the future of the business he felt the best decision was to fire the father-in-law but if he were to do so he would have a family problem because his wife would not like her husband doing so. The compassionate response was to find a respectful way to retire his father-in-law. By slowing down the transition and adding compassion the objectives of trusteeship were achieved without loss of value or creating family conflict.

National

At the societal level Enactus is doing a great job with its teaching and promotion of triple bottom line initiatives by university students around the world. As a judge at their world competition a few years ago I was delighted to see the millions of dollars raised and the millions of people served in projects that also helped protect the environment. The more we can do to focus on the importance of the triple bottom line the better it will be for all of us.

Another group I have worked with making an impact on society is called The Pachamama Alliance and their workshop, Awakening the Dreamer, most valuable in helping remind leaders to bring forth an environmentally sustainable, spiritually fulfilling and socially just human presence on earth. This mission is bigger than most organisations would ever attempt to undertake but at the intersection of these three spheres is the type of leadership that I am talking about when I refer to trusteeship and we really don't see enough of it today.

Aboriginal leaders that I have witnessed in northern Canada, South East Asia, South America and Australia are often cited as taking decisions based on what will be good for their grandchildren whereas business leaders in the markets today consider what is best for the share price this quarter. The difference between long-term and short-term is dramatic and the resulting decisions are quite different. We need only look at the state of the world today to realise the impact of the lack of trusteeship witnessed in the last twenty years.

As a boy scout I was taught to practice no trace camping and because of this I find it unfathomable to understand how people willingly leave behind their garbage on the ground after using public spaces for their pleasure. Whom do they think will clean up after them? Perhaps as one friend tells me, he leaves his tray behind in MacDonald's to create employment for people picking up after customers. The world however isn't MacDonald's and the following words, by poet Drew Dillinger, author of the poem Hieroglyphic Highway, remind us of our individual and collective responsibility at this pivotal time in human history:

"it's 3:23 in the morning
and I'm awake
because my great great grandchildren
won't let me sleep
my great great grandchildren
ask me in dreams
what did you do while the planet was plundered?
what did you do when the earth was unraveling?

surely you did something
when the seasons started failing?

as the mammals, reptiles, birds were all dying?

did you fill the streets with protest
when democracy was stolen?

what did you do
once
you
knew?"

Trusteeship supports environmental protection. The needs of our human population, which now surpasses 7 billion (a dramatic increase in my lifetime), means that humans everywhere are encroaching into the previously unspoilt regions on earth and in the oceans. Unless we learn to live sustainably, we are all doomed as we can see from the collapse of several species on earth, in our skies and in our oceans. This became dramatically clear to me when I was fighting fires in Alberta and our camp food was being taken at night by a nearby black bear. To protect our food, we hired a local native to stalk and kill the bear. He elected to sleep in my tent which opened with a perfect view of our food stores.

At 3:23am our sharpshooter awoke looking for the bear knowing they normally came scrummaging food just before dawn. As if on queue we awoke scared to death at the sound of the native's large rifle going off inside our tent where we all slept. Immediately our shooter told us the bear was dead and our food saved. It was not necessarily legal to kill black bears where we were, but the law of the jungle takes over in situations like this. After savagely taking our souvenirs (I took a bear claw) a helicopter was called in and a lynch lowered from the helicopter. We secured ropes around the chest and under the front legs of the 600-hundred-pound bear. Then signaling to the helicopter the bear was lifted high into the air, looking like a giant person flying. Once over a nearby swamp the pilot released the bear and dropped it directly into the swamp where its weight buried the carcass several feet below the surface never to be seen again. Was this the best option to protect our food and the bear? Obviously not and today it is safe to say a tranquilizer would have been used, the bear airlifted far away from our camp and deposed safely on the ground where it would eventually awake and carry on in its new corner of the forest far from the fire and from our camp. As man and nature clash more and more we are also becoming better trustees of our earth but our population growth and the lack of a trustee mindset in major cities around the world means we may be nearing the tipping point from which all of humanity will not return.

Solutions

Societal leaders are elected by the current population but should take decisions with future generations in mind. If we only think short-term, be it running up our credit cards, raping the earth or working deadly hours, we all lose. Be a trustee and then people will entrust their dreams and assets to you knowing you are not in it for personal gain but rather to help others over the long term. Trusteeship is linked to karma which suggests that creating merit by doing good will eventually be returned to you in terms of happiness in this or future generations. Monotheistic religions link the benefits of trusteeship to ascending to heaven rather than descending to hell.

So, what can we do to improve our trusteeship?

1. At the personal level I recommend reading about the principles of emptiness and craving after which you will surely come to the realisation that what really matters is helping others realise their potential and not accumulating material wealth

2. At the organisational level I recommend good corporate governance practices and corporate social responsibility also call ESG (environmental, social, governance)

3. At the societal level I recommend public servants eliminate all corruption and take decisions based upon what would be good for future generations, not what would be good for their bonus or what would get their party elected in the next election.

Open to Diversity

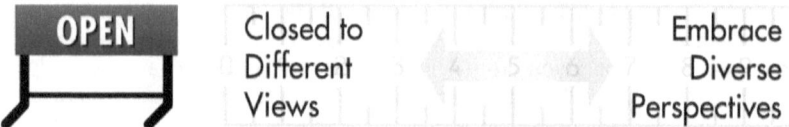

| OPEN | Closed to Different Views | | | | Embrace Diverse Perspectives |

"Strong cultures exist when employees are intensely committed
to a shared set of values and norms,
but the effects depend on what those values and norms are.
If you are going to build a strong culture,
it's paramount to make diversity one of your core values." (Grant)

Individual

Leaders open to diverse ideas and approaches succeed over those who are not. The complicated and rapidly changing world in which we live today means that no single person can possibly keep up to date on all the evolving risks and opportunities affecting them personally and collectively. To succeed today, leaders need the input of people close to the issues to conceptualise the implications and decide how best to respond.

To open yourself to being more accepting and understanding of diverse ideas and behaviours (like wearing a mask when you are around people in the midst of a pandemic) it is good to both study foreign issues and travel to understand the world. Having now visited roughly 60 countries and studied to understand the issues and people involved in the public and private sectors in all those countries I can say today that few of the beliefs I learned as a boy have by now been tested or changed entirely. Most people in the world do not have the chance to study and travel as I have. Leaders emerge locally with strong beliefs as to what they think is right and wrong. Often in the face of change people dig in their heels and reinforce their beliefs instead of suspending their beliefs (at least temporarily) to open a space for others to share their perspectives and understanding. Into this space can rush new understanding and learning resulting in change for good.

"The greatest tragedy of mankind," Dalio says,
"comes from the inability of people to have thoughtful disagreement
to find out what's true." (Grant)

I had the chance to work with the wealth management arm of a large UK based bank. They were hosting several of their high net worth families at a resort near Shanghai on Chongming Island (the site of fierce fighting with the Japanese in 1937 and held by them until 1945). I was invited to facilitate dialogue between the older and younger generations. The method I chose was Challenge Mapping. Once two groups were organized (basically parents or "senior generation" and offspring or "new generation") both groups worked on the question "How might we optimize our happiness and prosperity". As expected, both groups came up with many similar issues, but the senior generation was more interested in managing family security and the new generation were more interested in the acquisition of skills. Once each group had the chance to dialogue in break out groups, I brought both generations together to dialogue on the issues raised in caucus. Informally both generations pointed fingers at the other generation as being the cause for their problems but upon deeper reflection they began to realise both the senior and new generation needed to suspend their beliefs and become more open to the diversity of hopes and fears of the other generation. The solution was in the dialogue because this weekend when many conflicts were resolved, and issues understood.

> "Medicine is not an exact art, there's lots of uncertainty,
> always evolving information, much room for doubt.
> The most dangerous people are the ones who speak with total authority
> and no room for error."
> Jerome Groopman, Harvard Medical School

The results are not always positive. In dealing with the Asian Development Bank which is tasked with alleviating poverty, it became apparent that their policy and procedures were hindering their achievement of results. When burdensome policies were found to cause hindrance of results (especially in the procurement department) the departmental leaders dug in their heels and stressed the reasoning for their strict rules. These same leaders were not in favour of change even though technology has already changed practices at other development banks.

The problem was not the bank or its national customers; the problem was the individual leaders and their willingness to be open to new ways of doing and being. Apparently, the bank had been criticized for inconsistent project management and now the opposite was true – overly control oriented. The result of the closed mindedness of the current leaders simply meant that some of the private sector suppliers, many of which were considered best in class in their respective industries, refused to serve the bank, stating the overly burdensome bureaucracy and paperwork as compared with equal or better options for work elsewhere. The result meant that the development bank invested in less efficient solutions leaving less money than possible for alleviating poverty – its original mission.

> "The midpoint of a task is often the best time for a leader to institute change,
> as it's when groups become most open to originality" (Grant)

Organisations

I have worked with some amazing global organisations. They typically seek out diverse ideas to enable themselves to innovate, attract talent and remain competitive. One such organisation is Google. I met some of Google's senior executives together with other corporate leaders from Silicon Valley during a golf and dialogue day in Victoria, BC a few years ago, I was amazed how open the competing Silicon Valley executives were sharing and listening to each other's perspectives. They talked about failing early and winning sooner, of how the entire ecosystem allows the matching of ideas and capital at such a rate this one part of the world is greatly changing the rest of the world. Many of the tech executives had worked in multiple organisations and while some competitive barriers existed as to what could be discussed they were far more open than any groups I had seen in other parts of the world. They were excited for each other's success realizing that if one wins, they all win due to overlapping technology, suppliers, customers, and investors in Silicon Valley.

I have seen similarly effective openness to diversity working with leading schools looking for better ways to deliver education in Hong Kong's highly competitive international school sector. I have seen openness in airline executives facing tough competition from other airlines and I have seen it in the far reaches of a banking empire where executives in their home market in Europe have come to realise the need to change as Asia overtakes Europe in financial importance. I have also seen this openness to exist in the most competitive professional firms, again perhaps driven by tough competition but seemingly open to diversity with the goal of being #1 in their industry and markets.

> "The most creative fashion collections came from houses
> where directors had the greatest experience abroad, but there were three twists.
> First, time living abroad didn't matter it was time working abroad.
> Second, the more the foreign culture differed from that of their native land.
> The highest originality occurred when directors had spent
> thirty-five years working abroad." (Grant)

Does tough competition result in openness to diversity? Not necessarily but if I consider some of the organisations I have worked with where the leaders and corporate culture is more closed, I find another factor slipping in.

Monopolies tend by their very nature to be fixed in their ways and some of the public sector groups I have worked with seem immune to openness. When asked, some public servants say change only means more work and if they can keep things the way they are without any threat to their existence then why bother. One government department still insists on receiving documents by fax some 15 years after most organisations switched to email.

Another factor that seems to stand in the way of openness to diversity is the sharp conflict that can arise when new ideas are suggested. I saw this in vivid colour when asked by a university to share my experience introducing performance management. While it was clear, the university needed to change to climb the global rankings it was also clear that some very smart and articulate professors were very closed to the idea of performance management. As they made it known they were opposed the HR department ran in the opposite direction preferring instead to avoid the conflict (an issue of bravery addressed latter). I on the other hand bravely stood in the middle of the fire, as I had done in other organisations, realizing that naysayers need to share their opinions after which they tend to step out of the way and watch change take effect. If the changes poorly go the naysayers simply say, "I told you so". If the changes go well, you never hear from them again. While their lack of openness is in my experience to their disadvantage, their willingness to express themselves allows change leaders to better understand and manage the issues involved. "A complaint is a gift" some say.

I also witnessed closed mindedness in West Virginia where I had been asked to share my international negotiation experience. When what the audience saw was so different from what they experienced locally they concluded my best practices were not relevant. It is true Asia is an exceptionally long way away from these people who bought and sold domestically but two of the participants requested private sessions to explore their investments in China and clearly benefited. So, it is fair to say sometimes close mindedness results from people not being able to see or not being helped to see how the ideas being offered are relevant to them in their world.

> "The more successful people have been in the past, the worse they perform
> when they enter a new environment. They become overconfident, and they are less likely
> to seek critical feedback even though the context is radically different."
> Adam Grant *Originals* (New York: Viking, 2016), p. 54

I was asked to speak to the newly promoted top leaders of one of the world's leading investment banks. My message included best practices on how to manage their emotions and keep their head while all about them people were losing theirs and blaming it on them. In this situation, the corporate culture held up many examples of leaders who lost their heads and tended instead to scream, shout and lead others in fear. It was also clear that as newly promoted senior leaders they had not yet experienced the pain of the buck stopping on their desk. While #2 in the hierarchy it is easy to stay out of the heat of the kitchen but once promoted to #1 leaders have no place to hide and openness to ideas (and managing emotions) becomes critically important. On this point it is also good to remember that when you get stressed you tend also to narrow your focus and become closed to diverse ideas just when you need them most.

I have also seen closed thinking in situations where the local leaders say the global best practices do not apply in their culture (which reinforces my point of their unwillingness to open to diversity). I have seen this in Cantonese companies unwilling to work harder at something they historically succeeded at haphazardly. I have seen this in Korean companies where I suggested promoting more women to senior management (men would inevitably lose jobs). I have seen closed mindedness in sales organisations where past success leads the sales leaders to think future success does not require any change of behavior. I have seen closed mindedness in a listed manufacturer that hired a very results oriented leader from their main competitor in order to strengthen their competitive behavior only to see their rock star leader quit after only a few weeks realizing the corporate culture of non-competitiveness meant his peers were unwilling to listen to his suggestions. In all these situations closed mindedness prevented the organisations from opening to diverse ways of being that were enabling their competitors to move ahead of them one day at a time.

Organisations can also have problems internally where one group disrespects another and as a result the organization including its customers and employees all suffer less than optimal outcomes. One example that comes to mind is the continual challenge between the civil engineers building roads and bridges and the socio-environmentalists that challenge the development due to the disruption brought to the people and environment. If development banks find it difficult to open and engage diverse views and opinions internally, and these people have all the resources available to learn to do so, how can we expect people on the ground to make sense of this? A practical example is that when a new road is built into an area where no road was previously (e.g. to open access to a new market or mine) the next thing to come are the truckers. Then come the services to cater to the truckers including overnight accommodation and with that prostitution. One thing sociologists are conscious of is how new highways can also become corridors for AIDS and other sexually transmitted diseases if the development doesn't come hand in hand with local education for the people living and working along the new road.

As my driver sped along a brand-new highway in Burma's north from the new airport to the ancient temples of Bagan, I looked at the changes afoot along the road sometimes with sadness as the beautiful country side was cut in half with the ribbon of concrete but also, I was happy knowing the general welfare of the people living along the road will, like everywhere in the world, improve with time, despite the risks.

Being open to diverse ideas also involves how organisations accommodate outsiders who come along and see things the locals cannot see because they lack the clarity that comes with working in different places and time. This was the case when I landed in Hong Kong in 1989 and asked my employer why we were not teaching Mandarin classes. The local leaders looked at me with surprise since Hong Kong's handover to China was still many years away and in living history Hong Kong people fled the mainland and its language to make their lives in Hong Kong speaking Cantonese. Sure, enough however within just a few years my employers had completely changed course because they now saw a rich future working with Mainland companies. Mandarin language courses became commonplace not only in our firm but in companies right across the territory. One entrepreneurial friend of mine even went as far as to set up a Mandarin language school which he subsequent sold to become a multi-millionaire only to later repurchase the company and do so again.

People who see technological change before the rest of us also remind us of the importance of being open to diverse ideas. This was the case in two situations involving my railway clients (KCRC and MTRC) which both faced the same changes simultaneously. One change involved the use of Hong Kong's Octopus Card, a tap and go stored value card that works on all public transit and in retail shops in Hong Kong. The technology was sound and the benefits significant but even though Hong Kong was one of the world's early adopters there were still naysayers who at the time saw no value in such change and were even unwilling to look at doing a pilot survey. In the end persistence by Hong Kong's major public transport operators was all it needed for the card to launch and thousands of retailers to jump onto the system once they saw the obvious benefits of doing so.

Another change at that time involved advertising on the train cars in Hong Kong. Anyone travelling in Hong Kong today would find it hard to imagine a time when there were no advertisements on the rail cars or station platforms because now advertising is everywhere. Like the adoption of the Octopus Card, first they tried a few advertisements and when no one complained they continued. Now paper, panel and even video advertisements are everywhere in trains and stations in Hong Kong (making it harder and harder to achieve mindfulness in transit).

> "Starting in 1981, the Macintosh team had begun granting an annual award
> to one person who challenged Jobs –
> and Jobs promoted every one of them to run a major division of Apple" (Grant)

I define culture as the ideas, customs, and behavior of a people in each time and space. This explains why two young Korean girls facing the societal obligations and restrictions placed upon them in traditional Korean society chose significantly different paths. Let us call the girls Kim and Soo. Kim opted to go to the USA for university where she learned English fluently and eventually found work with a US multinational in California. Soo opted to stay in Korea for university and because she performed well in her exams Soo was offered a job and joined the country's #1 accounting firm, the local subsidiary of one of the world's Big Four firms. Soon after joining her US multinational Kim accepted an offer to move to Seoul and take up a senior position with the same company there.

I had the good fortune of working with both Kim and Soo's employers on separate assignments during the same month and it was there I met these two lovely women. The difference between the two could not have been any starker because despite coming from basically identical childhoods their university years and choice of employer had completely changed their outlook.

Kim loved being back in her country and free to excel in her employer's organization regardless of being female. She was already recognized as one of the highflyers. Soo however despite being equally talented was growing increasingly frustrated by the glass ceiling and traditional roles relegating women to second class citizens in traditional Korean companies. Seeing Kim's contribution to her US employer and knowing Soo's wasted potential in her Korean employer, I suggested to the main board members of Soo's Korean company (all male in matching black suits) that they should promote females to the upper echelons of the firm or risk losing them to more progressive employers. Their initial reaction was to thank me and do nothing. As talented ladies began to leave to greener pastures the all-male board promoted Soo, but she soon left as well. Why? Opening to diverse ideas and perspectives is more than just lip service, you must be seen to embrace diversity and even if you do not make changes you must dialogue with the stakeholders to fully explain your thinking. If they accept your thinking, they will continue to follow you but if they do not, they will either leave or turn off their effort and simply coast inside your organization. There are many people coasting today. Soo was too ambitious to simply coast so when she saw the men had little regard for her ideas she resigned.

To ensure that authentic dissenters voiced their viewpoints earlier, Bock's team created the "Canaries" – a group of trusted engineers across the company who represent diverse viewpoints, and have a reputation both for being sensitive to adverse conditions and for speaking their minds. They took their name from the nineteenth-century practice of using canaries to detect deadly gases in coal mines. Before Google's people operations team introduces a major change in policy, they often run it by the Canaries for critical feedback. They are part advisory board, part focus group, and they have become an invaluable safeguard to make sure Googlers' voices are heard. By reaching out to them in advance, one member of Bock's team explains, "Our biggest complainers become our strongest advocates." Adam Grant *Originals* (New York: Viking, 2016), p. 198

National

At the national level, the democratic system allows for change but leaders who are re-elected to office and remain popular over time are open to diversity and do not force situations into black and white decisions. When Singapore began searching the world for ways to become more creative it did not get bogged down in the endless discussion of whether it was already creative. When the popular Canadian Prime Minister Justin Trudeau was asked why he was naming an equal number of men and women to his federal cabinet his simple response was "because it is 2015". He was simply saying that the close mindedness of previous generations regarding equal rights for women was not something that he shared. The population sighed relief and moved on to other issues. Oman, when compared with other countries in the Gulf, pays more respect to other religions than do its neighbours. This respect is not to the detriment of Islam and is simply a reflection of the country's openness to diversity.

Another example where the difference in openness is apparent is when you compare quasi-government or government linked organisations with their full government counterparts. The government linked companies, partially impacted by market forces and responsible for profit and loss, want to be open to diverse ideas knowing this helps them achieve their mandate.

"The people here are very conservative and strongly object to any innovations.
Their invariable answer is that their fathers and grandfathers always did it this way,
consequently it's good enough for them.
Suggest the most simple improvement to them and one that they can see

and admit would be an advantage, but you get the same shake of the head
and 'my father didn't do it....'" (Gittins)

So, what explains governments that are not open to diversity? Hong Kong's unwillingness to engage student opinions during their Umbrella Movement, the chill that followed the Arab Spring, the treatment of English in the French province of Quebec, Britain's desire to exit the European Union, fundamentalist terrorism that scars cities around the world and public servants who refuse new topics to be discussed at public meetings if the issue isn't previously approved for inclusion in the agenda (no surprises) are all examples of people challenged by diversity.

China's invasion and cultural genocide in Tibet does not bode well for the future of the regime because their lack of respect for one of the world's greatest cultures hurts China in every imaginable way. Although China says it respects its minorities and puts several languages on their paper currency it is the Han Chinese majority followed by the Shanghainese, Cantonese and other leading Chinese dialect groups which control the levers of power. It is only in places where central control is not in majority that they are having problems such as Tibet, Xinjiang, Taiwan, and Hong Kong. I have spent days living and talking with the Tibetan refugees in India, Taiwanese nationalists in Taipei, Cantonese localists in Hong Kong and Uyghur refugees in Canada. Only once Beijing's leaders truly demonstrate they value and respect the diverse ways of being that exists amongst the over 1 billion souls that inhabit its territory, will China really become the world leader that it strives to be.

"The more we cling to the identity of our own group,
the more we need to demonize other groups.
That demonization, oddly,
becomes strongest the more similar us-and-them are". (Goleman)

I was just six years old when my parents took my brothers and I to the opening of EXPO '67 - the World Fair in Montreal. It was heady times for Montreal and Canada and people that visit Montreal today joke that locals still talk about it as if it were yesterday. Until the 1970's very few people had the chance to visit other countries so it was only by visiting exhibits like the World Fair where people could learn firsthand about different cultures and nationalities. Canada at the time was also learning to deal with the growing French unease inside the English-speaking country. At about the same time the country became officially bilingual and espoused a policy of multi-culturalism suggesting that people could live side by side peaceably in Canada much like the pavilions stood side by side at Montreal's World Fair.

Today multi-culturalism has been superseded by what sociologists are calling inter-culturalism and the difference is an important one. Whereas in the past people from different cultures could live as neighbours without much overlap now healthy societies involve people of different cultures living interspersed and interacting and understanding each other. Now people share and celebrate each other's cultures and in so doing the openness to diversity enriches the society. Perhaps it is easier for me to say this is a good idea because I have been lucky to globalize my personal experience faster than the world was globalizing itself. Perhaps it is more reasonable to see the opening to diversity more like a scale from closed at one end to respectful in the middle and sharing and celebrating each other's ideas at the opposite end. One thing for sure, those who are open to diversity are amongst the leaders and those who are not are falling further behind each year.

> "The Communists have to use lots of censorship,
> which is actually a sign of their weakness
> – it shows their fear, that they have something to hide.
> Our side is completely transparent.
> These are some of the reasons we never lost hope." (Goleman)

Solutions

In all the above cases my experience tells me that the fear of losing control is stronger than the desire to be open to new ideas and ways of being. This loss of control can arise from several places but again from my experience it typically arises from one of three places:

1. Insecurity in leadership e.g. they fear they will lose their job

2. Lack of knowledge, skill, or experience on how to do things differently e.g. they fear others will be more competent or needed to help current leaders

3. Unseen reasons making it more advantageous to continue than to change (e.g. corruption) – making leaders unwilling to discuss any ideas that might eventually lead to unwanted change

So, what can we do to improve our openness to diverse ideas?

1. I discussed studying and travelling the world, but this takes time and resources not everyone has. Another idea is to simply use the people around you from all over the world and ask them for their perspectives about how people in their cultures approach or think about certain topics. Most of us live in remarkably diverse neighbourhoods so engaging in dialogue and asking questions about things you do not know about can quickly give you insights you never imagined.

2. At the corporate level I have found compassion to be the best solution because if closed mindedness arises from either insecurity or ignorance the only way you learn about this is by showing your compassion and (privately) helping the leaders in question. Corporations also invest in opportunities for their senior executives to network and access executive education where they can learn what is going on. It is important for companies to do this and it is important for executives to take advantage of the opportunity to do so. If you find yourself in a company that does not invest in, you nothing prevents you from doing it yourself. It will be one of your best investments ever. Likewise, the internet makes accessing such information even easier. Leverage social media and you will begin to see things you need to know come into your in-tray daily.

3. Finally, the most important thing in the public sector is to lead by example realizing everything you say and do is magnified hundreds of times to those looking at you. Suspend your thoughts of what is right and wrong and open to diverse ideas by engaging with all stakeholder groups. Not only will you learn important things you need to know, you will also be showing others the importance of doing so. If you are not convinced just think of the racism and violence that spreads when leaders espouse hate towards certain groups in society. If a leader talks about racism today this escalates into people acting on his/her words. Knowing this it is important leaders set a positive example instead. Readers need only consider their experience with US

President Donald Trump whose lack of openness to the realities of the pandemic has left too many of his countrymen dead and sick while his divisive tone on the issue of Black Lives Matter has simply enflamed more violence.

Partner

Loner	Collaborator
Unreliable	Unifying
Isolated	Team Player

"Building walls... is a kind of folly that ought to be exposed for exactly what it is, namely a delusion that can neither be made fully to work in theory or in practice. Ignorance of the other is not a strategy for survival." (Shehadeh)

Individual

Another cultural hurdle for success today is our ability to partner with others. At the individual level think about marriage, the emotional rollercoaster of love which combines family, project, and financial management with living together to meet personal and family expectations of "happily ever after". With all the things that can go wrong during a marriage, it is no surprise that half or more marriages end in divorce and that there are more people than ever living alone.

Effective partnership does not have to mean forever to be considered successful because after all nothing is forever. Successful partnership should instead be measured as to the productivity, creativity and harmony experienced during the period you and your partner(s) chose to be together. If you think of music bands some simply play covers together while others play, create, and become famous together. During the life of the partnership it is inevitable that productivity, creativity, and harmony will ebb and flow but if the relationship is good for those involved partnership is better than splitting up.

Some people are better at giving and receiving in partnerships while creating value and harmony together. We all know people that are great to be with and others who rub you the wrong way. There are several reasons why some people partner better than others. One reason is that your motivational type might conflict with that of your partner as in the example below. Another reason might be the person's life experience never involved sharing or surrendering personal needs in favour of others. A third reason preventing successful partnership is differing objectives or values. It is wise to explore all three issues before launching into a partnership with someone be it at home, at work or in society.

To deal with motivational differences, psychometric tools can help you better understand your style and that of others and to learn how the differences both attract and repel some people. The tool I find most effective in this regard is the Strength Deployment Inventory (Scudder) which my clients have found extremely helpful in diagnosing motivational preferences and learning how people with different preferences either come together or clash depending on their styles. This tool is also highly effective at exploring how motivations change as you or your partner(s) get stressed and problems arise.

Sports are a great teacher of teamwork and partnering. Some companies I work with value highly any recruits that have demonstrated excellence in team sports like rugby, football, and ice hockey because they know these people are real team players. My brother David played hockey in Canada at the varsity level and like my son Long Tim who plays varsity rugby, both have amongst their strongest traits that of partner or team player. When life deals the challenges, it does team players will typically do all they can to help you out. The same was evident when I joined the parents of Canada's women's ice hockey Olympic championship team at the 1998 Nagano Olympics. Although these girls mostly grew up playing hockey in the shadow of their brothers the partnership, they demonstrate with their teammates on ice is better than everything else. It is not surprising that Nagano started a historic run of success which has seen them win or place second in every world competition ever since.

> "We all play many roles, professional and personal, in one lifetime.
> A liberal education gives us a greater capacity to be good workers,
> but it will also give us the capacity to be good partners, friends, parents, and citizens." (Zakaria)

Organisation

One example that comes to mind was a situation I was asked to resolve in Thailand. A German boss had been parachuted into a Thai team to sort out production delays and get things working again. This leader had been successful everywhere he had previously worked, and the company had expressly selected him as the right guy to sort out the mess in Thailand. (He had never worked in Thailand, but he had holidayed in Phuket once).

Problems arose early however because the manager (Thomas - name changed to protect identity) found the more he pushed for results the less his Thai team members did anything. I was informed the Thai team was very unhappy with their new boss. Thomas told me he was considering firing the whole bunch of them. It was culturally apparent to me that Thomas' aggressive results-oriented style clashed 100% with the Thai's relationship oriented and comparatively less competitive culture. I realized it would be easier to help Thomas change than the Thai team since they were all Thai and they were living and working in Thailand. So, I explained to Thomas how his behavior differed from that of his team as well as the cultural origins of the differences. After a bit of effort Thomas changed and the problems disappeared.

It is hard to know about your partner's background, values, and objectives. To learn more about these you need to dialogue and question each other about your principles, values, concepts, and practices. For a useful exploration of this I recommend Tony Lendrum's *The Strategic Partnering Handbook*. Tony and I overlapped working for China Light & Power, one of Hong Kong's two electric power utilities and an organization interested in optimizing the value of partnership with their strategic suppliers. Tony also sees the direct link between culture and success. He writes:

> "Some would argue that the two major types of culture [corporate and national] are quite
> different and should not be confused...my view is that the two are inextricably linked. The
> country culture is born out of hundreds, even thousands, of years of history. Religion, climate,
> geography, politics, and time have shaped the basic values and beliefs of the society. It is
> impossible to imagine that these influences will not flow over to business in various forms. After
> all, it is people who lie at the heart of business, not machines. The culture of the organization
> must in some way reflect the culture of its surroundings." (Lendrum)

So, what leads some individuals to isolate themselves from their partners? I like the analogy of a relationship being like a zipper which works fine until a thread enters the teeth of the zipper and snags the tab preventing it from moving up or down. Relationships connect like a zipper in many ways (productivity (e.g. projects), creativity (e.g. innovations) and harmony (e.g. individual relations) over time and it is natural for snags to arise. Our ability to deal with the snags, to remove the blockages and allow the zipper to resume sliding up and down, is a big part of successful partnership over time. Likewise, people tend to remember all the times a snag arose in the partnership and these influence the effort people expend resolving conflicts that arise. The more past problems have left a scar the less partners are willing to try and solve new problems together. This is true at work, at home and in society.

I was called into one of my banking clients to help sort out a conflict involving one of the banks most productive financial experts – let us call him Abdul. Abdul's knowledge allowed his bank to create investment products that effectively made money for the bank regardless of the direction of the market. The only problem was that Abdul was infinitely smarter than the team he was given to work with and when his team members made mistakes (and lost money for the bank) Abdul was blamed. Abdul's view was that after he taught his team how to create the complex trades, they were responsible for they would forget important details and make mistakes. Rather than continue training and retraining he began firing people for making repeated mistakes (a normal response for many of us). When losses arose, he pointed out his staff's shortcomings but the more he did this the more his conflict averse face-saving team members hated working for him. Obviously, the secret was helping Abdul maintain his cool in the face of repeated mistakes and installing quality control mechanisms to prevent inadequately structured trades going live before getting corrected.

Upon investigation Abdul's lack of willingness to partner with the team he had been given was compounded by the fact he was treated like an outsider by his peers. This lack of partnership behavior by Abdul's peers was partly due to jealously about his outstanding financial results and partly due to his interpersonal style which was more highly strung and emotional than many of his cold rational colleagues. As problems arose differences were accentuated.

The solution to this situation involved recognizing that growing the number of Abdul's direct reports was not going to give a commensurate boost to the bottom line because of the team members inability to partner. Instead the bank accepted their inability to partner and established Abdul and the small number of experts he oversaw as independent experts all operating with their own budgets. Similar in a sense to how universities often deal with professors which are loosely affiliated to faculties but largely operate in their own spheres of influence. Subject matter experts, like Abdul, university professors, class teachers, lawyers, accountants, etc. often associate to share overhead costs like offices and administrative support but otherwise work individually spinning in their own orbits.

I am often asked why I declined partnership in my firm after spending ten years of my life working hard to achieve the goal of partnership. I learned a lot about myself in the process of those ten years including my strengths, weaknesses, values, and objectives. I had witnessed firsthand three different varieties of partnership – Montreal, Geneva, and Hong Kong. By the early 1990's accounting partnerships were in the throes of huge change. Partners' individual liability was sky rocketing, job descriptions were rapidly evolving and pay per hour worked was dismal when compared with directors of finance, consultants, and bankers. What finally helped me decide was not the working conditions or potential legal liability. I simply found that my basic values and objectives differed from those of my partners. I was starting a young family and wanted to spend time with my kids whereas my partners at the time were mostly either single or sent their children off to boarding school. While this was particular to Hong Kong at that time, I did not want to leave Hong Kong, so I opted instead to launch a consulting business with two of my partners with whom I shared more basic values.

My choice of partners in the early 90's was based on my fundamental values and objectives. With hindsight, had I accepted partnership with what eventually became the biggest accounting firm in the world, I'd likely be financially richer today but would certainly never have enjoyed the rich family, personal and professional experiences of the last twenty years. Every person must decide who they partner with when the time comes and finding a match based upon your motivational styles, values and objectives will always provide you with a sound foundation to weather the changes that will always come to test your partnerships. Linking up for financial reasons has not in my experience or that of my clients, proven to lead to long term productivity, creativity, or harmony. As discussed elsewhere in this book you and your partners should not only agree on what you do and how you do it, you should also agree on why you do it because why you do what you do is what will ultimately fuel the success of your partnership.

In the corporate setting, I, have found engineers, especially civil engineers to demonstrate better than average partnering behaviour probably due to the fact they must work together with other professionals to achieve the goal of their work i.e. roads, bridges, buildings etc. I have many examples of client off sites demonstrating successful partnering behavior because they arrange to meet with sister departments on whom they rely. For example, finance meeting with compliance or sales meeting with service. In these cases, successful partnership arises from the dialogue between the groups. Some companies are aiding partnership by putting "coverage officers" into other departments. For example, the HR department, instead of sitting everyone together in the HR department are choosing instead to sit their members into their "client" departments e.g. HR coverage person in sales, HR coverage person in operations etc.

My in-house client workshops are extremely popular when clients bring together the managers from different departments to adapt best practices into their situations and in doing so talk through the issues causing friction when partnering together. A data engineering company which I worked with recently identified interdepartmental partnership as their main hurdle to effective business development. When they realized they had 11 department heads in my workshop all agreeing partnership was their main problem I asked how often they normally meet as a group and the answer was never. It is important for companies to create a space in their busy agendas to dialogue and agree on ways to improve their partnering behavior. It is not hard, but it does need investment.

I have done hundreds of workshops around the world helping teams dialogue on the issues that matter. These sessions have helped companies better serve their customers (internal and external). For one organisation focused on supply management, the value created went directly to the bottom line and represented most their company's profit for several years. In other situations, they were better able to address competitor and market changes and align resources efficiently to maximize profits.

Corporate partnering is not always present or working well. Several clients point to the IT department as their worst partner. Another client is always asking me to "partner" by completing their on-line questionnaires. What is it that prevents these organisations from partnering successfully? In addition to partnership challenges arising from motivational style, relationship history, values and objectives, the following examples highlight a few more aspects of the hurdles we must overcome to partner successfully.

In Hong Kong I worked with two business schools which operate across town from each other and within the same cultural environment. I have noticed their partnering ability is significantly different and upon closer examination I believe the reason is to do with their leaders. In one organisation, the leaders reach out to find experts to partner with and enhance the overall product for their students. In the other organisation they see outside experts as threats to their jobs and costs in terms of their P&L. In both situations, the leader's partnering behavior (or lack thereof) was heavily influencing the rest of their team. Since Beijing has increased its influence on Hong Kong many foreign professors have been let go, some believing this was done intentionally to eliminate the risk of "foreign interference" in student's thinking.

In another situation in Boston where I was working with a defense contractor the leader was very abusive of their vendors. Team members said she was always like this but in my situation, I chose to discontinue the partnership. In all my years working around the world she was the most abusive client I had ever worked with. I have seen similar abuse in another situation, but I was not the subject of the abuse, my client was. In that situation, the industry leader was financially and emotionally abusive of their supplier. While the sheer size of the client made, the supplier wants to sell to them once they witnessed the behavior of the procurement team the supplier opted to stop selling to them. In this case the market leader's inability to partner with their supplier meant this key parts manufacturer was pushed to work with the market leader's main rival, an advantage one should never give to your competitor.

Sometimes partnering is interrupted when one partner takes an unfair share of the profit generated by the other partner. I have seen this in a few situations, one where an entire team of finance lawyers quit and joined a competing law firm. I can name several examples where clients realized the profits of their service providers was so high the clients decided to enter the market and offer the same service themselves effectively cutting out their partners.

A few situations of interrupted partnerships arise where one party focuses too much of their time on their own needs thereby ignoring the needs of the other partners. I know two managing directors that were fired for getting the balance wrong between their own needs and those of their employer. Sometimes these situations can also involve theft, either by the employee or the employer and I have seen both. Partnership, like marriage, is not about taking, it is about giving. I describe it like a glass of water. If you both pour water into the glass, you have a relationship overflowing with success but if you both take from the glass eventually you end up parched and wanting.

Several years ago, I facilitated a valuable career development session whereby successful leaders were asked to consider their career path and identify any common conditions present each time their career trajectory changed. In every case these successful leaders identified a valuable partner that helped them through the change by encouraging, questioning, referring, supporting, or even stopping them from taking a path that was not suitable for them.

Two of my clients build their business model on their ability to partner with the owners of the businesses which they manage on behalf of the owners. One is Marriott International, often cited as the best in the hospitality industry and the other is Caterpillar often cited as best in the construction equipment industry. Marriott manages hotels owned by other people. Caterpillar manages the heavy equipment business for locally owned distributors. In both situations over many decades both companies have proven the value of partnering.

"We are caught in an inescapable network of mutuality,
tied in a single garment of destiny.
Whatever affects one directly, affects all indirectly." (Goleman)

National

At the national level look at the most successful economies to see who is partnering well and then look at the most dismal economies to see who is not partnering well. Successful economies tend to partner well externally (e.g. Brexit vs EU, MAGA vs United Nations) and internally (e.g. partnership between the public and private sectors and between the federal, state, and local governments). Governments that are failing tend to suffer from an imbalance between the public, private, and tertiary sectors. Successful partnership at the national level can also arise from international assistance e.g. Cambodia's rise after the end of their civil war. The Asian Development Bank has plenty of successful examples of infrastructure built by foreign companies, paid by foreign countries, and benefitting poverty alleviation in developing countries. Foreign aid was paid when I was invited to help CGA Canada develop 1 million new accountants in China.

Nations also generate plenty of examples of poor partnership and for a few obvious reasons. In many countries, a psychological divide exists between public and private sector workers, one thinking they are only in it for the money and the other thinking they are only in it for an easy life. At the national level, it is easy to focus on the "in group" that is presently in power to the detriment of the "out group" that as minorities lack influence in government decision making. The UK's Brexit vote is a case in point of a group of people thinking it better to make it on their own rather than partner with others having different values and objectives. Governments must partner with every sector not only the ones that elected them or which they align with.

There is an endless list of failed states which focused on one group to the detriment of another. Nation building is not a zero-sum game. Helping all groups will bring you more partnering success than only helping a select few. Examples abound where groups overlooked have eventually proven to be of great value in another country. Political refugees to Western countries are often cited but think as well about today's Syrian migrants boosting the German economy or the Rohingya that will in time boost the economy of countries like Malaysia and Thailand to which they are fleeing from Myanmar.

I was only 15 when Montreal hosted the 1976 Olympics. The lead up the Olympics was a disaster for all concerned. Labour strikes shut down construction, schools, and hospitals across Quebec. The need to complete construction of the Olympic installations meant that cost overruns would bankrupt the city for the next 30 years. On top of this international tensions were causing problems for visiting teams.

My brother Bob took me along to witness firsthand as apartment blocks in the east end of Montreal burned to the ground while the fire services (who were on strike for higher wages) stood by watching the apartments burn without extinguishing the blaze. Another day, while my secondary school was closed for a teachers' strike I jumped on my bicycle and drove to look at the Olympic site and the wondrous stadium and velodrome that were being built 24 hours a day to meet the opening date of the games. The stadium roof and tower were only completed many years after the Olympic games. In the end the minimum needed was in place for the opening ceremony.

The complete lack of partnership demonstrated by the unions and national teams meant the 1976 Olympics almost never happened and considering they created the biggest financial deficit in Olympic history the lack of partnership affected future events the city was bidding on. If cities and states are to succeed today, they need all their main stakeholders working together in concert to compete with other destinations that are working harmoniously. While Quebec was holding one referendum after another to end their partnership with Canada, talent and businesses from all language groups were leaving the province for better places to work. I was travelling between Hong Kong and Singapore at the time watching these two competing cities vie for jobs moving to Asia to accommodate the growth of the region. It was at that time when INSEAD, Europe's leading business school, decided to upgrade its presence in Asia by building a bricks and mortar campus. As the story goes, they asked the Hong Kong Government if they would like to partner with INSEAD. Hong Kong's typical response was 'of course you have a free hand' (referring to Adam Smith's free hand of open capital markets and government non-intervention). Singapore on the other hand apparently said, 'yes we'll even give you a hand'. The difference between these two cities at that point, with Hong Kong offering to partner by getting out of the way and Singapore offering to partner by giving a helping hand, explains why INSEAD and many other employers have chosen Singapore over Hong Kong in the last twenty years. Leaders partner proactively and laggards do not.

The same can be said of Israel's partnering with the high-tech industry. When I visited SOSA, the business incubator in Tel Aviv, I was extremely impressed at how the start-ups were helping each other. Successful companies were partnering with start-ups, banks and government were helping and everyone had a direct link to capital raising on NASDAQ.

In 1989, while Ronald Reagan was calling on Mikhail Gorbachev to "pull down that wall" separating east and west Berlin, Margaret Thatcher and the British Government placed ropes along the Spree River behind the Reichstag building so that if East Germans were brave enough to swim to freedom on the western shore they could grab a rope to pull themselves out of the river (rescuers were not allowed to enter the river to help them and many people died trying to cross the river during the years the city was divided).

In 2013 I was lucky to achieve one of my life goals being to visit South Africa while Nelson Mandela was still alive. Although long retired from politics he was still an icon of partnership and hope for all South Africans. Through sheer conviction and leadership, he convinced the warring tribes that made up Black South Africa to work together with their white enemies, the ones who had subjected them to years of persecution under apartheid, because he knew that only together could all South Africans build the rainbow nation he and others envisaged. Mandela won their partnership, despite the fact it must have been terribly hard at times, knowing anything less would lead to failure.

While the South African Government's willingness to partner ebbs and flows so too has Hong Kong's. My small consultancy is systematically audited every seven years to ensure I am paying the right amount of tax. As a CPA I make sure to keep my books up to date while taking advantage of Hong Kong's favourable tax structure. I have now been in business long enough to enjoy three tax audits by Hong Kong's Inland Revenue. Despite the fact my business has never changed and nothing incorrect has or will be found to exist, the audits themselves have become increasingly difficult each time. Although my company's tax audits might have become increasingly challenging because of what they have found hiding in other similarly organized businesses, I think it is mainly because of their declining willingness to partner with the auditee. I was an auditor myself for ten years and continue to train auditors and I know that as an auditor if you don't partner with your auditee to achieve your audit objectives you waste time and resources and sometimes don't meet your audit objectives.

The first time I was audited the tax auditor invited me to meet him and explain my business. Everything was in order and following lunch together everything was signed and sealed. The second time I was audited I was not invited to meet them face to face and the auditor kept asking for more information each time I answered his questions. Too busy to handle the details myself I hired a tax consultant to deal with the Inland Revenue. The third time my business was audited it became apparent they had learned little if anything from the first two audits, they never asked to meet me and their questions indicated a lack of understanding of my relatively simply business model. The result of Inland Revenue's inability to partner with my tax accountant or I led to months of delay and sub-optimal outcomes for all. Sometimes when you want to partner and the other party doesn't it can be very frustrating but as my tax consultant confirms, relationships matter in partnerships and the fact Inland Revenue changed their auditor every time and weren't interested in meeting us is part of their problem.

> "Those who try to make life better for everyone
> without having learned to control their own lives first
> usually end up making things worse all around." (Csikszentmihalyi)

Solutions

So, what can we do to boost our partnering behaviours?
1. At the leadership level I recommend learning more about your own and your partners' motivations, partnering history, values, and objectives

2. At the corporate level, you should consider all your leaders and their influence (good or bad) on others. You should also create space and opportunities for partners to dialogue on the issues that matter. Networking is useful to get to know your partners better and

training in teamwork will help develop more of the positive behaviours required to make partnerships work.

3. At the national level, you should do those things listed above but also ensure that all peoples are included because excluding one or more groups for whatever reason (linguistic, racial, religious, political, gender etc.) means you will be achieving a sub-optimal outcome. It can be helpful to research partnerships inside your community to identify which groups and organisations are connected and which are not. One particularly useful software tool for this can be found at the University of Colorado Denver http://partnertool.net/about/ .

Bravery

Risk Averse	Courageous
Avoid Conflict	Smart
Avoid Responsibility	Negotiator

> "Of all the virtues we can learn, no trait is more useful,
> more essential for survival, and more likely to improve the quality of life,
> than the ability to transform adversity into an enjoyable challenge." (Csikszentmihalyi)

Individual

In 2016 Hong Kong bookseller Lam Wing Kee became famous for bravely explaining the truth behind his detention in China. He had been told he could visit Hong Kong to collect the names of his bookstore customers and return to the Mainland to assist them with their crackdown on books critical of current Chinese leadership. Following eight months under detention Lam followed the orders of his minders, travelled to Hong Kong to collect the database containing the names wanted by the authorities and began his return trip to China but on route to the border he mustered enough courage to leave the train before arriving at the Chinese border. He then contacted his lawyers who arranged a press conference where he told the truth about what had happened to him.

What caused Lam to speak up when all the other booksellers detained in China and returned to Hong Kong agreed to remain mute on what had happened to them during detention in the mainland? The common response is that the others still have family members on the mainland and thus the cost of bravery would be too high. Lam says that when he learned thousands of people took to the streets of Hong Kong to protest his release, knowing of their support gave him the strength needed to courageously speak up. He eventually fled Hong Kong and now runs a bookshop in Taiwan.

Individual examples of bravery take place every day and vary in context from seemingly small things like speaking up in a meeting to major stands of bravery like that of Lam. Bravery in Asia's conflict avoidant culture is relatively rare compared to America's *stand up and fight* culture. In Confucian societies people are taught from a young age not to raise their head above the crowd and thus, when it comes time to get the issues on the table, so problems can be resolved and innovation created, the need for courage exceeds that seen in organisations today. Sometimes bravery arises from individual passion or mission but for bravery to be exhibited more often, individuals like Lam, need to feel the support of people who agree with their positions.

> "The reasonable man adapts himself to the world;
> the unreasonable one persists in trying to adapt the world to himself.
> Therefore, all progress depends on the unreasonable man." (Grant)

I visited Dharamshala, the exiled home of His Holiness the Dalai Lama at the same time the 100th Buddhist monk or nun had self-immolated in protest to China's repressive regime in Tibet. To most of us it is shocking to think someone could be brave enough to set themselves alight in respect of their beliefs. I seldom see acts of bravery that approximate self-harm in companies or government but courage to express oneself in hope of changing things for the better (I am not suggesting self-harm) is needed to achieve optimal outcomes.

I'm often asked about the bravery it must have taken me to jump from my assured work as an auditor to the itinerant work of consultant, the former guaranteed work through statutory requirement and the later needing to find work on a regular basis. There is risk with every job. Before becoming an accountant, I worked as a forest fire fighter in Alberta battling fires like the one that engulfed Fort McMurray in 2016. Interestingly changing from forest fire fighter to accountant I went from one of the most dangerous jobs to one of the safest. Fires were scary but training and safety measures kept us out of trouble normally. One of the more worrisome situations was when one of our senior forestry leaders got drunk and began marauding dangerously with a gun. Fortunately, we used remote radio connections to track his whereabouts and kept away from him until he passed out without harming anyone. Once again, the solution was in the dialogue. While bravery is important, proper risk management and training is essential. I turned down promotion to the rap attack crew before turning to auditing. This crew was the best regarded fire fighters in the province, but the job description did not fit my level of bravery where you purposefully jump out of helicopters into forest fires to rapidly extinguish the flames ignited by lightening.

"In every domain, from business and politics to science and art,
the people who move the world forward with original ideas are rarely paragons of conviction
and commitment. As they question traditions and challenge the status quo,
they may appear bold and self-assured on the surface.
But when you peel back the layers, the truth is that they, too,
grapple with fear, ambivalence, and self-doubt." (Grant)

When I left the comfort of my audit firm one of my partners in Singapore said, "I shouldn't stay out too long because the longer you stay out the harder it is to get back in". This partner could not imagine "life on the outside" and feared for my future. Sadly, his fear was to return and haunt him because some years later when his firm merged with a competing firm he was let go and without bravery to find new work he simply retired early foregoing years of potentially well paid work. Sometimes bravery is proactive and sometimes it is needed in reaction to life's twists and turns. Either way, as the 1873 hymn *Dare to be a Daniel* (Bliss) reminds us:

Dare to be a Daniel
Dare to stand alone
Dare to have a purpose firm
Dare to make it known

One question that often arises is whether you should leave a bad boss if you have a good job. I learned early that you are only as good as your boss so unless there is potential for your boss to move on in the near term you are best advised to get the experience and exposure you want and then move on yourself remembering your bad boss as an example of what you don't want to be like yourself in the future.

"Great spirits have always encountered opposition from mediocre minds." (Grant)

Organisation

Thomas Campos, a smart passionate alumnus of Bishop's University, interned with me in Hong Kong. After he left, he eventually joined a small start-up called Uber which has quickly revolutionized the taxi industry around the world. Uber believes change is needed and local people want a better choice. I first used Uber in Thailand when I landed in Bangkok and needed a ride out of the city. The experience was so much better than all other alternatives that it is a wonder how any government can willingly hold back this improvement. Uber is creating an interesting clash between the public and private sectors in all the markets where the local taxi industry has risen to withstand the competition. Public servants however, in office to serve the will of the people as directed by their elected ministers, need to find their way bravely through the turmoil.

An interesting example of bravery arose when the Director of Finance for one of Europe's leading airlines was asked to purchase used jet fighter aircraft at above net book value thereby creating a profit for the government in need of surplus. This transaction had two problems, firstly civilian airlines do not need air force jets and secondly accounting principles suggest you should not pay more than net book value unless there is good reason. Recognising obvious reasons to say no to this transaction the director of finance bravely rejected the deal knowing it would result in his being fired from his job. He was fired and a replacement was found who signed off on the deal. While the former director of finance can be credited for his bravery, his replacement can be questioned for the basis of his decision. It is easier to stand firm when you believe in your reasoning. If your decision is based on self-benefit you can be sure that you will be found out eventually, your staff will at best stop supporting you and at worst rally to get you removed.

"Before you criticize people, you should walk a mile in their shoes.
That way, when you criticize them, you're a mile away and you have their shoes". (Grant)

In Kuala Lumpur I met a brave employee of Exxon who was attending a change management workshop I was invited to lead about their merger with Mobil. This petrol-chemical engineer, having served the company for twenty years, bravely and loudly so all could hear, described my change management workshop as nothing more than making employees happy before selecting which would be fired given the merger would create two people for every one job. If economies of scale were to be achieved, then headcount reduction was needed. Thanking him for his bravery in expressing his emotion I asked the group to take a time out and in private realized he had already decided to retire rather than work through the merger. I invited him to stay for the workshop (he was going to walk out) and apply all the change management principles to changing from employed to retired. He agreed and by the end of the day said it was the most valuable day of his life. While he was brave in expressing his emotions, I too showed bravery in confronting and de-escalating the situation head-on. Avoidance would have never achieved the optimal outcome which the soon to retire engineer attested to at the end of the day.

This experience served me well when I was leading a workshop in Bahamas for a merchant bank. Soon after introducing the workshop (on negotiation) one of the senior bankers shouted out that my workshop was a waste of time and he and others would leave. Again, I interrupted the planned session to address his obviously strong views. In his opinion and that of others in the room the bank's biggest negotiations were not external with clients but internal with the credit committee which regularly turned down most of the new business the bankers were proposing. Every time the credit committee declined a deal the potential business went to a competing bank and the banker having spotted the opportunity not only lost his/her commission but also suffered the resulting relationship problems with their client. Because of this newly discovered problem I bravely adjusted the training to focus on the credit committee and internal negotiations rather than external client negotiations. The result was outstanding because it allowed for improved internal negotiations and the learning impacted the external negotiations as well. In time this bank improved its client book to such an extent that it was sold to an acquiring bank from Qatar for significant multiples.

> "Venting doesn't extinguish the flame of anger; it feeds it.
> When we vent our anger, we put a lead foot on the gas pedal of the go system,
> attacking the target who enraged us". "Venting doesn't work even if you think it does
> – and even if it makes you feel good.
> The better you feel after venting, the more aggressive you get:
> not only toward your critic, but also toward innocent bystanders".
> Adam Grant *Originals* (New York: Viking, 2016), p. 240

Hong Kong offered the world a European example of conflict avoidance when the French perfume brand Lancôme cancelled their sponsorship of Denise Ho's Hong Kong music concert at short notice following Beijing's expressed displeasure about Denise Ho's involvement in the Umbrella Movement. Whether the reason for their cancelled sponsorship is true we may never know but in terms of bravery Denise Ho came out on top when she continued with her concert as scheduled at her own expense and thousands of people protested the Lancôme brand.

Another lack of bravery case I am working on involves two business partners that long ago fell out and now really do not like each other. Separately they want to sell their shares and divest of the company but collectively they refuse to do so preferring the trouble they know with each other to the unknown future that awaits them if they sell their business. In their case the lack of bravery perpetuates their sub-optimal situation and prevents the opening of a space for new opportunities to arise. As they say when you close one door another will open but when you fear closing the door the opportunities awaiting you will remain unseen.

National

In Bahrain during the civil unrest that pitted the majority Shia population against the ruling Sunni leadership I was introduced to government leaders in the hope of sharing ideas that could help reduce the domestic violence and replace it with dialogue to overcome the issues unsettling the general population. One result of this unrest was the introduction of the Manama Dialogues, a brave attempt at getting the stakeholders around the table to discuss regional security concerns.

The challenge for corporations and governments is to face up to change and bravely leap into the unknown. In the private sector risk is better understood and rewarded but in the public sector the opposite is true and few if any public servants are rewarded for taking risks. In fact, those bravely venturing outside of existing policy and procedure, even when it makes sense, are often demoted, or moved to new responsibilities immediately.

"Ultimately, the people who choose to champion originality are the ones who propel us forward.
After spending years studying them and interacting with them,
I am struck that their inner experiences are not any different from our own.
They feel the same fear, the same doubt, as the rest of us.
What sets them apart is that they take action anyway.
They know in their hearts that failing would yield less regret than failing to try". (Grant)

Young people are relatively more courageous than older folk. Some suggest this is because young people have less to lose or because they have yet to experience the extremely negative consequences of risk taking gone wrong. I taught students that were in Tiananmen Square, lived in Europe and witnessed firsthand the crumbling of the Iron Curtain and walked the streets talking to young people during several long nights of Hong Kong's Umbrella Revolution. What I witnessed in all these situations was not a lack of awareness of the risk or having little to lose, what I witnessed was a bravery arising from the inspiration of wanting a future different from that painted for them by society at the time.

In June 2016 when the youth of Britain voted to remain in Europe while their elders voted to leave (Brexit) it gave me yet another example of youth taking a little more risk (remain and try to make things work) because they had the longest future ahead of them. In opposition, elders who had witnessed Europe before the EU and were taking perhaps the easier route by voting to cut and run hope things will improve with little downside. Risk tolerance involves being very well informed of risk before venturing into the unknown. Scenario planning, rehearsals, crisis management policies and stress testing are all important parts of the picture for individuals, organisations and governments that demonstrate a higher level of bravery and thus higher level of success. These courageous leaders understand they need to "fail often to succeed sooner" as the product designers at IDEO taught us. These leaders also learned early that "nothing ventured, nothing gained". Mindfulness, dialogue, and risk management must underpin a culture of bravery otherwise change will lead to more bad outcomes than good.

A few examples of a lack of bravery will help you understand where I am coming from. When my book, entitled *Dialogue Gap,* became popular there were requests to translate it into Chinese. Due to Confucian teaching deeply embedded in Chinese families, and problems resulting from our misuse of digital communication, skills and methods needed to overcome the effects of dialogue gap are in demand in the Chinese speaking world. When I accepted to proceed with the translation, I anticipated problems passing the Communist party censors in Beijing. My references to the Dalai Lama, Tibet, Taiwan, Tiananmen, and whistle blowers, which collectively represented only a few of the 200 pages in the book, were sure to cause alarm and the first translation was refused. When asked if my publisher's translators could "cleanse" the book and remove the offensive references, I confirmed it would not hurt the integrity of the book and that because the people and organizations of China were expressing a desire for the solutions I was offering, they could proceed with the "cleanse" and resubmission.

On first submission, I anticipated problems because of the Communist Party's desire to remove all traces of negative stories from local readers' eyes. When the manuscript was resubmitted a second time, I anticipated problems again but for a different reason. The second submission would need to be reviewed by the same government body that reviewed the first submission and because of a lack of bravery it would only take one person on the committee to decline the application and the Chinese edition of Dialogue Gap would be killed in China. Sure enough, the decision was negative, and no further reasons were given. Culture reared its head to prevent an optimal outcome. Surprised? No.

> "In the long run, societies based on submission
> generally find themselves at odds with natural human impulses." (Zakaria)

In Singapore I take great pleasure running the annual *Conflict & Emotional Literacy Workshop* for the Singapore Institute of Management (SIM). Singaporeans, per Hofstede's study, are the most conflict averse (or least brave) of all groups studied. There are many reasons for this but what is interesting is that Singaporeans work in some of the most advanced companies in the world and must deal with big problems but with relatively less experience in conflict than people elsewhere, hence the training. What Singaporeans do not learn at home or growing up they are more than willing to learn in executive education especially when the training is practical and can immediately relieve them of stress they are suffering on the job.

I could go on and on about fear of intervening to change and the lack of bravery preventing change from happening. Perhaps the last example I can offer at this stage is that of an international law firm operating in Tokyo. The firm hired me to arrange an offsite to address the major issues facing the firm in Japan and come up with strategies to achieve the goals for the coming few years. As I do each time I prepared for the offsite in some detail and got up to speed on all the major issues they were facing. All that was needed was to design a day that would help the people involved achieve their objectives. The day was going well but by two in the afternoon we still hadn't addressed what I knew to be the "elephant in the room" namely an issue specific to the firm in Japan but to which no one wanted to speak. Realising that conflict aversion and the importance of saving face would forever prevent the topic from being raised I stepped in as someone from outside of the culture and put the issue on the table so it could be discussed. After a silent pause people jumped onto the issue and aimed to resolve it. Had I not bravely put the issue into the open I think they would still be stuck with the problem today. In this case, it was my experience that gave me the bravery to put forward the issue for discussion knowing the solution is in the dialogue.

Early in my career, in a similar situation working with a Hong Kong Government department, the strategy offsite was ending and the yet unnamed "elephant in the room" was that their boss was micro-managing and all the problems were arising from her micro-management. My problem was that the micro-manager was my client and my lack of experience meant I lacked the bravery to tell her she was the problem. The issue was never made explicit nor dealt with properly, so the person retired, and the strategic objectives ended up being fulfilled by her replacement. Since that day, I will never avoid the tough conversations. The battle weary tend to be the bravest not because they like battle, quite the opposite, because they hate to see the negative outcome of not resolving problems before they blow up in your face.

I was working in Bangkok leading a large workshop with several hundred people at the time of one of Thailand's recent military coups. This serious situation which arose without warning meant that several hundred foreigners from across Asia were holed up in the hotel awaiting news about their safety. It was interesting to look at the audience from the perspective of risk avoidance and bravery. The company decided to help arrange transport to the airport and flights back to their home countries for all the participants who feared for their lives. The only participants that opted to leave Thailand were the Chinese from China and Hong Kong who imagined the worst by referencing the June 4th massacre in Tiananmen Square. All remaining participants, including non-Chinese from China and Hong Kong, chose to remain and the workshop continued. The people choosing to remain all came from countries neighbouring Thailand and had personal experience where risk assessment combined with a higher risk tolerance enabled them to stay on and complete the workshop safely. Some like me even ventured out into the streets to take photographs beside the tanks on Sukhumvit Road.

> "The world is a dangerous place to live;
> not because of the people who are evil,
> but because of the people who don't do anything about it." (Goleman)

I cannot leave the topic of bravery in the national context without touching on two of the toughest situations in the world today. The first of these is the reality of Palestinians and Israelis sharing the same land – Palestine. Since the creation of Israel this challenge has gone unresolved and while everyone has attempted to solve the problem of co-habitation the conflicts persist. I visited Israel recently and engaged in dialogue with a member of the Knesset, a retired general of the Israeli Defense Force, a Palestinian who had witnessed countless killings in the occupied territories and a Jewish émigré extremist happy to reclaim their promised land and take up residence in the beautiful homes being built inside the walled oasis beyond reach of the local Muslims who have worked the land and their olive trees for generations. This life and death open sore for mankind began in the Holocaust and Nakba of the 1940's. The bravest people I have met are not the Jewish settlers or the Israeli army officers raiding the camps or Palestinians fighting for their land. The bravest souls I met included both an Israeli Rabbi and a Palestinian Freedom Fighter that had become friends realizing the only way a solution could be reached was by working together, not killing each other. I was so inspired I thought it would be great to bring these two leaders to Malaysia and begin sharing more of the truth of the situation with those who can help influence the global forces behind this seemingly endless conflict. Unfortunately, Malaysia does not allow visitors from Israel nor does it allow its own citizens to visit peoples. I am optimistic the future will open to diversity and allow for dialogue between these countries.

The second example of bravery is related to the above situation. When I had the opportunity to visit Iran, I was asked to advise a senior advisor to the Ayatollah on their negotiations with the USA. As a condition to entry to Iran we were asked not to speak about religion or politics but here I was being asked directly for advice on both. Perhaps the people of Iran believed my surname Nixon suggested I had some inside knowledge of USA politics or perhaps the then recently released movie depicting the role of Canada helping American diplomats escape the Iranian revolution suggested Canadian passport holders were American citizens. Either way I could advise on such a complex issue but what I could and did say was that the Iranian president needed to stop saying Israel should be wiped off the face of the earth. This was brave but it is also true, and truth gives you bravery. My questioner thanked me, and I have not subsequently heard the president repeat this line. Iran and the USA are now enjoying their best relations in decades and the world is welcoming the Persian Empire back to the community of nations.

> "Act now and persist.
> Act even if the cause seems hopeless –
> and never give up" (Goleman)

As we watched the youth of Hong Kong put their futures on the line in the name of democracy we watched bravery in the raw. Many called this stupidity. Regardless of which side you consider yourself to sit in this matter, individuals, companies and nations are for the first time in decades putting their beliefs ahead of economics, something many of us wondered if we would ever see it again. This latest era has led to a lot of conflict and it is important to combine bravery with wisdom and an ability to dialogue and overcome differences. If our leaders cannot overcome these hurdles and focus on potential rather than money or control, the next few years will do little to solve the bigger problems we are facing in terms of health and climate.

Solutions

So, what can we do to increase our bravery? Here are a few ideas:

1. Personally, you should be constantly widening your comfort zone, trying new things, and giving yourself a challenge. Since these things will lead to stress and sometimes conflict you should learn and practice the 40 conflict de-escalation tactics which I include in the appendix of this book.

2. Organisationally you should encourage people to speak up and when they do you should thank them and tell them what you are doing with their suggestions. Reward people for coming forward with ideas, suggestions, complaints, and challenges. You want to know about these so that you can help take corrective measures and optimize results.

3. In society, it is important that government genuinely listen and be seen to be listening to all their stakeholders. Listening is not enough though and as the feedback loop is shared governments must also show what has been learned and done because of the feedback. This isn't a popularity contest and governments can't possibly act on all recommendations so even where things are not done governments should explain why and then in time and through democratic processes people can attempt to elect delegates to get what they want or realise their original demands cannot be met or are not significant enough to warrant the resources required.

Negotiation requires bravery to get what you want personally and organizationally. I suggest becoming adept at negotiating. You want to become a star negotiator managing the content, process, and people in your negotiations. For further tips on negotiation and culture I suggest reading my book *Negotiation: Mastering Business in Asia*.

Finally, it is important to mention that many of the bravest souls in history stood strong beside their beliefs for ethical reasons seeing themselves as defenders of right and wrong. Although there is and will continue to be endless debate between the various religions in the world, it is useful to look deeper at the underlying ethical considerations and decide for yourself what you believe. Only then will you be able to take a stand in those grey situations where decisions are not black and white and can go either way. Brave leaders need to take a stand and live by the consequences. A recent example of this was Britain's Prime Minister David Cameron who fought hard for Britain to remain in the European Union but when he lost the Brexit referendum he resigned as Prime Minister. He bravely stood by his conviction that remaining in the European Union was the best choice and in doing so he was willing to surrender the job he had sought his entire life to fill. The UK is still sorting itself out of this Brexit situation two Prime Ministers later.

Cost need not be high when you stand your ground but if you rise to relatively senior ranks in either the private or public sector you will always encounter situations requiring bravery and the cost of your decisions will grow in both importance for others and consequences (good and bad) for yourself. As they say in the Boy Scouts – **Be Prepared**.

Another aspect of bravery is being in tune with yourself, with your emotions and with the world around you. When I chose to put aside my audit career to try my hand at consulting it was a brave move on my part made easier because of the time I had taken to become alert to my own goals and ambitions and how the world around me was evolving with a dying mother, a growing family and significant changes amongst my partners and the profession. Looking back, it was indeed a brave move (I even lay in bed at night sweating with worry at the time) but I would have never achieved what I have achieved today had I not taken that leap of faith at that stage of my career. My mindfulness was crucial at that stage as it is for all successful leaders, organisations and governments and this is the next cultural hurdle which I address.

> "What people enjoy is not the sense of *being* in control,
> but the sense of *exercising* control in difficult situations.
> It is not possible to experience a feeling of control unless one is willing to give up
> the safety of protective routines. Only when a doubtful outcome is at stake,
> and one is able to influence that outcome,
> can a person really know whether she is in control." (Csikszentmihalyi)

Alert

Distracted	Mindful
Distant	Focused
Unsatisfied	Content

"When we are in the grip of anger,
most of the negatives we perceive are wrong:
Ninety percent are mental projections." (Goleman)

Individual

Covid'19 was first discovered by the WHO through monitoring China's medical announcements online. Being alert personally and organizationally can even save lives. I was invited to speak to a woman's group in Hong Kong's financial district. My honorarium included a book voucher at one of the local bookshops. Since I was enjoying a free read, I decided to find a book from a section of the bookstore I seldom visited – religion - and by chance came upon a book entitled *Destructive Emotions* by Daniel Goleman. As I was familiar with Goleman's work in *Emotional Intelligence* and because destructive emotions are a common problem in negotiation the book intrigued me. I bought the book, took it home and had it read in just a few days. I was hooked. In Goleman's book, he described a series of dialogues between Western Scientists and Buddhist Monks exploring parallels between the findings of modern brain research and knowledge refined from over 2500 years of Buddhist studies and research. This book opened a door for me to learn and begin applying the teachings of Buddhist philosophy and many of its practical tips which I share to de-escalate conflict (see appendix). Mindfulness, a common buzzword which directs people to this body of work, started thousands of years ago, and extends to this very moment in research and practice at work, at home and in society.

By mindfulness I refer to being fully present, alert, and aware of what is happening in and around you. This awareness not only enables you to manage accordingly but with regular practice it leads to improved emotion management, happiness and decision making. Mindfulness practice is working its way into schools, offices, and governments to counter the digital onslaught of information that interrupts our consciousness and shortens our ability to focus. As people lose connection with themselves and their surroundings they are more easily distracted, unhappy and feel like they are living on an emotional rollercoaster.

All extraordinarily successful leaders that I have had the chance to work with do something to regain and strengthen their mindfulness daily. Some meditate, pray, or take time off during the day in silence. Some go for walks or runs often in nature. Some enjoy hobbies like gardening, painting, or music. Senior leaders do not have a lot of time but through regular practice even a short refresher can reset their minds into the calm, serene, focused state typical of mindfulness. This quick synchronisation can be done looking at a favourite picture on their phone, engaging in dialogue, or focusing compassionately on the people they work or live with. My favourite activities are walking in nature and listening to music. These two activities usually help me regain a serene and focused mind and when in this state, I can work productively at my desk for hours writing, reading, and handling client matters effectively. When I have not practiced for some time I will anger more easily, and I notice that cognitively I am not operating at my best.

When young I thought nothing of mindfulness and do not believe that I was particularly effective in this regard. In secondary school, as I sat trying to do my homework, I was unable to sit still and focus for more than a few moments before my mind would wonder off to another topic or my hands would start moving. The interesting thing was that the more I sat and tried to focus the longer were the intervals between distractions. Today much is known about neuroplasticity and our ability to improve our cognitive functions. Despite this new-found knowledge (in Western Society) our laptops and smartphones are simultaneously reducing our ability to concentrate, and some say we are living in a society suffering from attention deficit disorder.

In Hong Kong, it is frustrating to walk on the sidewalk because today people walk looking at their smartphones rather than the street in front of them and the people around them. Since it is safer to walk in the middle of the sidewalk when not focused on where you are going and since it is impossible to read and walk well at the same time these people slow down effectively blocking the walkways. Up in the board rooms overlooking the streets of Hong Kong executives are effectively doing the same thing, looking at their phones rather than mindfully engaging with their work and the people with whom they are meeting. The results of this lack of mindfulness are apparent in poor decision making, reduced employee engagement, increased conflict, and lack of commitment.

When my three children were young, we found ourselves moving often to keep ahead of Hong Kong's rising rents. At one point, we had the chance to move into a lovely garden flat, on December 26th. To make the move special I arranged for each of our children to receive their first bicycles which were assembled and awaited them in the living room of our new place. The joy on their faces was worth the effort but to understand my link to mindfulness I invite you to consider the man from whom I bought the bikes. This man had a young family and he and his wife earned a small amount of money renting bicycles to tourists at the corner of the beach at nearby Silvermine Bay. He spoke little English and I speak little Cantonese but mindfully I had noticed his young children and wanted to help him by giving him some business. He likewise remembered me because my wife and I had rented bikes from him before and mindfully he noticed our three kids two of whom are Chinese and adopted in Hong Kong. Because of our mutual mindfulness, we could negotiate the sale and purchase of three assembled bikes even though as a hirer of bicycles he had never sold bikes before. In the end, he understood that like most fathers I too wanted to impress my children with their own bicycles.

"Unless one learns to tolerate and even enjoy being alone,
it is very difficult to accomplish any task that requires undivided concentration." (Csikszentmihalyi)

Organisation

Mindfulness at work is gaining a lot of recognition and converts but Muslims, because people take regular prayer breaks, are in my experience amongst the more focused people in workplaces. Some of the wealthiest and most modern organisations are fitting out their offices with physical places where people can recluse themselves for some quiet time. Likewise, schools are beginning to recognize the value of such spaces in their classrooms (for younger children) and on their campuses (for older students).

Google has become famous for its in-company mindfulness training which has now spread to other companies and is written up in the bestselling book *Search inside Yourself* (Tan). In this course, employees learn to slowdown and focus their attention resulting in better decision making, improved interpersonal relations, improved people management etc.

> "Creativity is allowing yourself to make mistakes.
> Art is knowing which ones to keep." (Grant)

I worked with the China practice representing a famous European wealth management firm. In my experience they were the worst group of executives I had ever worked with. They seemed totally uninterested in the topic of the workshop despite the fact the Human Resources department had extended the time available for my session once they realized I could address more of their business development needs than originally thought. The China practice was hemorrhaging cash and they needed to improve their client relationship skills. In the wealth management business asset management is built on good relationships, ability to dialogue and sales negotiations. These are all built on being alert and mindful when in conversation with prospective clients.

The problem with this group, from the leaders right through to the most junior members, was that they were completely unfocused, uninterested, and undisciplined. Not all the executives that day were problematic, and one or two that showed terrific promise and responsibility saved my session from what could have been a disaster. Following the session, I contacted the Human Resources department to do a debriefing, but they were not interested. This is normally a sign HR only wanted to tick a box and not really make an intervention to improve the organization.

I then reached out to the best of the participants, their top sales executive, to share my feedback about the group and see if I could help further. He responded thanking me for the feedback but saying he was leaving the team and returning to Europe (he obviously saw the problem too). Within a year, the China team were all fired, and the office closed. The famous European wealth manager had lost millions on their China venture and I was able to see it in less than sixty minutes.

What was their problem? Attention. The China executives, trying to keep track of their clients and markets at the same time, ended up losing their ability to be alert to anything. They made mistakes, were unable to build relationships, sustain dialogue with prospective clients and negotiate sales. Their lack of mindfulness was their undoing. The bosses in Europe did not spend enough time in China to mindfully see the problems. The good sales executives sent to China from Europe just figured it was a cultural issue. The Chinese executives were to win new business from Chinese clients while the European sales executives in China were there to serve their European clients. The problem was the China team and I saw it in no time. Knowing this, the next time I see a problem like this I will be bolder to warn them collectively and not only rely on talking to HR or their effective sales executives.

National

Secular societies are struggling with the concept of mindfulness, some confusing it with religion and others with yoga (which was invented to enable people to meditate longer without feeling uncomfortable sitting long periods). In deeply religious societies mindfulness is compared with prayer or sitting in silent contemplation with God. In Penang I was enjoying a World Music Concert (pre-pandemic) when the music was halted to allow for evening prayer. We are still working out how and where to work mindfulness into our lives but clearly modern research and historic traditions all point to the value of taking a time out and enjoying a quiet time where you can order and then wipe away your thoughts to address and stabilize your emotions and become one with your surroundings to regain your presence and your attractiveness as someone to work with in harmony for the good of the world around you.

Mindfulness includes being mindful of the issues and trends affecting the people in your network. When Hong Kong recently announced their drive to improve innovation, I wondered what they were thinking about twenty years ago, when I was invited to Singapore to address the same question. Singapore, then under the leadership of founding father Lee Kwan Yew, mindfully recognized the future of Singapore lay in Singaporeans ability to reinvent themselves and that innovation was lacking. Through various initiatives Singapore has effectively blossomed into the leading city state that it is today. While Hong Kong was then focused on transitioning to Chinese rule it is now mindfully recognizing that it has fallen behind competing markets and that it must now focus on innovation as a matter of policy. As Singapore realized, this change does not come easily but mindfulness on behalf of the leaders and the people is an essential starting point for effective social change.

It is easy to identify examples of mindfulness lacking in both the corporate and public sectors and an easy time to see this is when planned change goes wrong. One of my clients that was preparing itself for takeover by a competitor did all it could to "pretty itself up" for takeover. Once a suitor was found the strategy was announced to the staff who were shocked thinking, they were working for an organization that was not expected to change its shareholding in any significant way. The directors, not mindful of how their key staff would feel watching their bosses' cash out of the company leaving them behind to work for new masters, were surprised when the takeover failed in the due diligence stage. This triggered the departure of all key staff not covered by fixed terms in the company. Once the key staff had resigned the attractiveness of the company dropped even further in the marketplace.

A lack of mindfulness seems to have been affecting the leaders of the ruling Conservative party in the UK when they chose to call a referendum over leaving or remaining in the European Union. Surely if they were mindful of the consequences of a failed referendum, which meant exit and is what happened in the end, they would never have chosen to hold a referendum in the first place. What causes this lack of mindfulness and how can you improve it personally, organizationally and at a societal level?

> "In ancient Egypt, there were two different verbs for *procrastination*:
> one denoted laziness, the other meant waiting for the right time". (Grant)

Solutions

1. I recommend daily meditative practices – whatever works for you and take as much time as necessary to regain your emotional balance. Some say the busier you are, the more time you should take to meditate. It is also particularly important to turn off your digital toys from time to time to give yourself uninterrupted time for you and your brain. Families can also enjoy a "quiet time" together for example sitting in silence together watching the sunset.

2. Organisations are bringing mindfulness training into the workplace, e.g. Google's *Search Inside Yourself*. Individuals and organisations can dive as deeply as they want into this subject as there are numerous levels of mindfulness which can be attained with regular practice. What companies should be aiming for however is at least ensuring their employees can stop and think long enough to work, decide and act effectively together with their colleagues.

3. At the societal level I think it is important to promote dialogue BEFORE decision making and to stress the importance of presence in dialogue. Companies and communities should also ensure enough parks and community spaces for their people to safely sit and recollect themselves amidst their hectic schedules of daily life

> "A good education system must confront the realities of the world we live in
> and educate in a way that addresses them,
> rather than pretend that these challenges don't exist." (Zakaria)

Dialogue

Uniformed	Informed
Small Network	Engaged
Don't Ask	Connected

"Hofmann found that a culture that focuses too heavily on solutions
becomes a culture of advocacy, dampening inquiry.
If you're always expected to have an answer ready,
you'll arrive at meetings with your diagnosis complete,
missing out on the chance to learn from a broad range of perspectives." (Grant)

Individual

In 2012 I published my second book – *Dialogue Gap* – to focus attention on the problems arising from our quickly disappearing ability to converse, a basic and uniquely human skill that has guided humanity right up until we put smartphones in everyone's hands and enabled them to communicate on everything imaginable 24 hours a day, 7 days a week. As I point out in Dialogue Gap, communication and dialogue are not the same. The former is to send information and the latter to resolve problems, innovate and learn. Problems began arising when people began communicating when they should have been in dialogue. Thus, at this moment in history when we should be better off than at any time in human history, instead we are confronted by historic levels of conflict, forced migration, global warming, economic distress, and political and family strife.

"Dialogue must begin, first of all, within oneself.
If we cannot make peace within,
how can we hope to bring about peace in the world?"
Thich Nhat Hanh

Mindful leaders recognise Dialogue Gap and put in place training, policies, and methodologies to overcome the problems arising from a lack of quantity and quality dialogue. At the personal level leaders are turning to available solutions such as executive coaches and HR to sort through their issues. The smart ones are joining forums (e.g. EO, YPO/WPO, Chambers of Commerce etc.) where they engage with peers from other organisations or departments on issues that matter. Unfortunately, most leaders today, especially the younger ones, either do not recognize the value of dialogue or find it hard to connect with others who similarly lack dialogue experience and skill.

The reaction to the Dialogue Gap book was overwhelming and an affirmation of the problems I witnessed and see getting worse around the world. In the old days people could come to the table and talk through their problems and arrive at a mutual agreement. During the last twenty years, I have witnessed a diminishing desire and ability to dialogue and resolve problems face to face. The many conflicts we face today are testament to dialogue gap.

Our dialogue research (the on-line survey of our client data base in connection with the release of *Dialogue Gap*) reinforced the existence of problems:

1. 100% of schools, companies, and government overlook dialogue training but,
2. 96% say we need more dialogue in society
3. 91% say we need more dialogue at work
4. 85% say we need more dialogue at home
5. 79% say it is a common, serious, or disastrous problem that we send information (e.g. text or email) when we should dialogue
6. 76% say a lack of dialogue is the cause of our problems in society
7. 72% believe others are losing the ability to dialogue
8. 67% say it is a common, serious, or disastrous problem that we forget to dialogue when we need to
9. 61% say a lack of dialogue is the cause of our problems at work
10. 48% say a lack of dialogue is the cause of our problems at home

A friend of ours has reached the mandatory retirement age but wants to keep working. Unfortunately, she has worked her entire life in a relatively narrow environment and for only 1-2 employers. While she is very competent at her job, she has a small network of friends, a limited knowledge of the industry and seemingly less knowledge of possible employers. Not wanting to reflect on the puzzle facing her and unwilling to network and dialogue to create options she had no choice but to take the first offer which came along following her retirement which was simply to work part time with her old employer. As an energetic sixty year old her skills and experience are in great demand in the industry but not necessarily with her employer. Unfortunately, her unwillingness to dialogue and her lack of courage to take the time required to explore options has left her with a sub-optimal outcome, less pay and benefits for effectively the same hours worked (the difference between fulltime vs part-time salary packages).

"A related method of learning through the ages
has been something that is often thought of as pure pleasure – conversation.
"Conversation," a former president of Yale, A. Whitney Griswold, wrote,
"is the oldest form of instruction of the human race,"
defining it as "the great creative art whereby man translates feeling into reason
and shares with his fellow man those innermost thoughts and ideals
of which civilization is made." (Zakaria)

Organisation

My friend Mack oversees ancillary services for a medium size university in America. Mack realized that the books he used to purchase as a student for $30 now cost $300 each despite the fact the cost of distribution of book has fallen greatly with the advent of eBooks and digital readers. Students and parents are angry at the escalating costs of textbooks and study packs, most of which are still paper bound and heavy to transport. Professors constantly complain about their pay packages and the profits arising from their textbook and study pack sales represent an important part of their income. Since the professors can basically control demand they issue a "new edition" each time they run the course and thereby eliminate the second hand textbook market telling students they need the new edition if they want to get a good grade. Meanwhile bookstores are facing increasing costs and to meet profit expectations are further increasing prices while reducing stock costs by minimising inventory. To further complicate matters Mack realized the publishers are reeling from the arrival of eBooks and the relative ease at which eBooks can be shared free further reducing unit sales.

Mack engaged me to help his small team dialogue and surface the key issues to find a way forward. To protect confidentiality, I will not go into the details of this case but rather share the first step which was to fill in the dialogue puzzle. As the picture below shows, Mack and his team had to respond to the puzzle in front of them:

1. **Outcome** - They needed to dialogue and consider what the optimal outcome would look like if indeed they could achieve it.
2. **Stakeholders** - They then needed to identify all the key stakeholders involved in this case e.g. students, parents, professors, publishers, printers, bookstores etc.
3. **Issues** - Once the stakeholders were identified Mack's team needed to identify all the key issues involved in this case e.g. cost to students, profit for professors, intellectual property rights, distribution costs, quality of content, new editions, availability in paper and digital formats etc.
4. **Way, time, space** - Only then, once the above three questions were answered could Mack and his team consider alternatives available within the culture of the university as to how, when, and where further dialogue could take place.

Leading businesses have figured out the great importance of dialogue, both internal and external. I have been fortunate to work with some of these leading organisations. In Hong Kong I facilitated a few sessions for the partners of an international search firm. This firm has been successful over many years, but their annual partner meetings featured more communication than dialogue, but both were needed. As a classic matrix organization leader from industry and country verticals needed to communicate what they were doing and with whom to ignite opportunities for other markets. Dialogue however was needed to allow the leaders space to think together and come up with innovative solutions to the advent of on-line competition like LinkedIn which was eating away at their non-retained and less senior search markets. Some participants said the ensuring dialogues were amongst the most valuable they had ever participated in during the last twenty years. Why assemble if not to dialogue? If it is only to communicate then send a memo. If you are getting people together you want to ensure it is to dialogue on the issues that matter.

"Argue like you're right and listen like you're wrong." (Grant)

One of my clients is a privately held family run business. Like all family enterprises the business sometimes suffers from the family issues arising between parents and children, or between siblings or cousins. Dialogue in non-family led businesses do not suffer the lapses caused by the jealousies, favouritism and incompetency issues which are normal and commonly tolerated inside family run businesses. To minimize the impact of these family issues some family offices rely on trusted advisors such as lawyers, accountants, bankers, and consultants, some working as independent non-executive directors in the family business. One of the main contributions of these non-family members is their willingness to state the obvious and force family members to discuss issues without the emotional baggage which typically builds up when people grow up together under the same roof.

Sadly, outsiders find it difficult to overcome the family issues standing in the way of sensible business decisions because at the end of the day families tend to take decisions which are best for the family versus what is best for the business. If you are in just such a situation I encourage you to put the issues on the table, arrange for the stakeholders to talk about them and then unless you are in a position of power in the family, stand aside and learn to live with whatever is ultimately decided. This is not to say that you should not hold your ground but in the end just like any organization if you can't live with the decision then you need to get out of the way, step down or relocate, because families evolve over generations slower than most businesses require to stay competitive.

Another place where dialogue is working its way into organisations is when activists focus the world's media onto a specific issue, e.g. environment. They tend to narrow the recommended decision to something black and white which the masses understand, and then turn up the heat for the leaders to succumb to the wishes of the activists. When the cause is popular, this is a highly effective tactic, but what effective organisations are doing is ensuring no surprises. They are engaging with their opponents on the issues that matter to the activists to influence the outcome from the earliest stages. If things must change, e.g. sale of cigarettes, companies need to be involved from the beginning and not ignore or ban or censor the topic simply because it goes against their stated objectives. When I worked with Phillip Morris in the 1980's they were already planning for changing consumer views towards smoking. Similarly, when the Royal Bank of Canada was being attacked for their financing of companies damaging the environment, they too were deeply involved in the conversation knowing exactly which investments were affected and assessing their risks accordingly.

Whether you are a public or private sector leader you must engage in dialogue on the issues that matter to you and your stakeholders whether you agree with them or not. Failure to do so will leave you blind to the issues and late to figure out how to respond. The solution is in the dialogue.

> "In a rapidly changing world, the lessons of experience
> can easily point us in the wrong direction.
> And because the pace of change is accelerating,
> our environments are becoming even more unpredictable.
> This makes intuition less reliable as a source of insight about new ideas
> and places a growing premium on analysis [and dialogue thereof]." (Grant)

My university work has highlighted an interesting dichotomy where faculties that dialogue and partner with the private sector (e.g. engineering, medicine, law, business, architecture) tend to be considerably more successful than those faculties that don't (for whatever reason) connect with the world outside the Ivory Tower as often as others (e.g. science, arts, education, religion). My observations working with roughly twenty or so universities around the world have also taught me that the difference between successful faculties is not the subject matter but rather the faculty leadership's willingness to dialogue with the outside world for research, hiring, fundraising, recruiting or placement of graduates. Continuous dialogue is what prompted many to jump wholeheartedly into online learning, while others became confronted with this do or die reality when the pandemic forced the closure of universities and colleges around the world.

At the individual level people often get promoted into positions of leadership based on their hard work and these same people quickly come to realise that the skills which got them promoted are different from the skills which make them successful as leaders. Dialogue and negotiation skills are the most important skills a leader can learn. If they have emerged from a family and work environment where dialogue was absent, they will find it exceedingly difficult to overcome this hurdle.

In my book on dialogue I list 50 dialogue skills. I recommend you identify which of these skills you should focus more attention on to become more effective as a leader. The skills fall into five categories with the acronym PRESA:

- **P**resence – the importance of being fully present and alert when in dialogue with others
- **R**espect – the importance of showing respect for people to open and share their views with you so you know what is really going on
- **E**xpression – the ability to express yourself effectively and get people you work with to do the same
- **S**uspending – the ability to put aside your own beliefs, assumptions, and ego to open a space into which you can begin to see the world through the eyes of other people and in so doing enhance your own understanding of the reality of the situation
- **A**bsorb – your ability to observe and listen deeply (and help others do the same) to pick up and comprehend all the messages (most of which are non-verbal) being communicated by the people around you.

Let me give an example. I was invited to be an advisor on the board of a financial institution that was preparing to list on the stock exchange. The company was founded and led by an incredibly hard driving and successful businessman who famously had a history of success as an Olympic athlete. As I and the other advisory board members sat through meetings listening to this CEO and his team we became increasingly concerned about a few aspects of the dialogue. One thing we noticed was an absence of clients visiting the company offices. Another thing we noticed was a continuous preference to dialogue about strategic opportunities for the business rather than the actual details of the business currently being faced. Sometimes advisors are used for considering future scenario planning and helping lift the leadership team members up and out of the day to day issues to consider the way forward. One thing however that was very noticeable was the CEO's inability to suspend his opinions about certain topics, after all he was the expert and the founder. If he had doubts, he might feel his leadership might be questioned. But this is exactly my point. In his culture leaders always know the way and tell followers to follow. As advisors from around the world we knew CEO's could not possibly always know the answer and that the solution is in the dialogue. Surely one of the most important aspects of an advisory board it to give the boss the space to challenge and be challenged. This lack of suspending on behalf of the CEO and his leadership team meant the advisory board was relied upon less and less and not surprising (but very unfortunately) the organization collapsed because of the senior leadership team's assumptions being wrong. Do not wait for your assumptions to catch you out. Suspend and dialogue.

Most work today is project based and dialogue is central to successful project management. As the two scenarios in Appendix 3 suggest, (10 steps to project crisis vs project success), dialogue is needed to succeed, and the absence of dialogue is commonly the cause of project failure. Knowing this we wonder why more companies do not focus more attention on getting the dialogue right.

"In our own lives we can opt for dialogue instead of conflict.
We can lengthen the pause between impulse and act,
taking time to think about what we *really* need in the long run.
Of course, a dialogue does not mean we will all agree, the Dalai Lama acknowledges.
"We have different views; there will always be disagreement.
You need patience but not a foolish patience,"
…but dialogue, not violence, is the answer,
"Invariably, violence creates more problems than it solves.
The only way to solve problems is not by the use of force but by talking

...that's why I say the coming years should be a century of dialogue." (Goleman)

National

Government leaders are learning the importance of dialogue as a method of resolving conflicts and achieving optimal outcomes at the national level. When the USA avoided dialogue and even insulted the WHO, Covid'19 cases sky-rocketed in their country. All that was needed was the ability to listen to the WHO, other countries rocked by the pandemic early in the spread and listen to their own CDC doctors to prevent the infections and deaths that spread like wildfire through the USA. The dialogue also needed to escalate the risk of local transmission up to the highest levels of the US government. And to make matters worse we see the USA retreating from dialogue in several multi-lateral organisations, the WHO included.

When I used to work exclusively in the private sector I shared the view of many in the private sector that government "bureaucrats" worked much less than people in the private sector and enjoyed benefits without the risk of market forces. While this might be true to a certain extent, my work with governments in the last decade has given me a completely different view. The major problems facing the world today are being addressed by public servants everywhere. They are doing their best (with few exceptions) and for the most part they chose to be public servants to leave a positive mark on their societies.

I have helped public servants improve dialogue in Malaysia, Iran, Singapore, Hong Kong, USA, Brazil, and Canada. There are interesting dialogue initiatives in these countries. In the southern Brazilian state of Rio Grande de Sul they famously invented *Participatory Budgeting*, a way of inviting citizens to dialogue on budget allocation decisions and a methodology being adopted in other parts of the world. In Sechelt, a municipality on Canada's West Coast, I facilitated a week of dialogue on the issues faced by both the local government and private sector leaders resulting in one of their best sharing sessions designed to help attract investment and settlement into their community. In the USA I witnessed the *National Coalition for Dialogue and Deliberation* (NCDD) dialogue on inner city revitalisation issues facing parts of Seattle. In Bahrain I helped key stakeholders explore how to handle civil strife issues resulting from favouritism of one group over another (a problem common to many countries). I did the same in Singapore where they held sessions called *Singapore Conversation*. In Malaysia, with the leadership of the Razak School of Government we have facilitated dialogue on cultural preservation and urban development as well as crisis relief resulting from man-made and natural disasters.

Not all governments are interested in dialogue and China's current government is one such example. To keep control of a country with over a billion people the Communist party keeps a firm lid on dissent by controlling all media. The Chinese translation of my book Dialogue Gap is banned in China (and presumably now in Hong Kong) because of references I make to their dialogue (or lack thereof) with Taiwan, Tibet, whistle blowers etc. No doubt this book will be banned too. As someone who has lived half his life in what is now Chinese territory (Hong Kong) I sincerely want to see China succeed but nothing I have learned in my work and travels around the world tells me censoring dialogue leads to optimal outcomes. Clearly China has created unprecedented value for its citizens by bringing hundreds of millions from illiteracy and poverty into living in the second largest economy in the world today. That said it is still obvious that there is a lot of dissent bubbling just under the surface in China and if they are to become more successful, they will need to harness this energy rather than attempt to bottle it. Only then will China be able to overcome the pollution, corruption, and spiritual vacuum plaguing Chinese society today.

Solutions

In your dialogue scenarios, I encourage the following solutions:
1. Use the Dialogue Puzzle to diagnose the stakeholders, issues, optimal outcome, and strategy to achieve it.

2. Employ dialogue skills (PRESA) effectively to engage the stakeholders and find out their needs and wants so you can respond to these accordingly.

3. Choose the right dialogue method for the outcome you want to achieve. Fifty dialogue methods are described in detail with links in my book *Dialogue Gap*. Rather than detail dialogue methods here I simply encourage you to read my book.

"By thinking of humanity as one – us –
we can better enter into conversations and negotiations that will leave everyone winners.
Dialogue is not a luxury we may choose to enjoy, but a simple necessity." (Goleman)

Faith

 Pessimistic   Optimistic
Overwhelmed   Resilient
Dependant   Confident

"If we have a long-term goal and we see that we're advancing toward it,
even if it is one tiny step at a time, it makes a big difference.
If it is a short-term goal, and we're just doing it to stop something,
or we're protesting from anger, then it never goes anywhere.
So finding that joy has been my solution.
"Almost every activist I know is actually an optimist at heart:
Your really have to believe that the society will be better off,"
Dekila added. "I think there is a natural ebullience,
an enthusiasm that comes from inside.
We're convinced, not matter what the odds are, that we will win." (Goleman)

Individual

How many people feel optimistic about the future given the current state of the world? This current situation is a true test of our faith. When I launched my business in the early 90's my wife was pregnant, and we were in the process of adopting our second child (Long Tim). What that meant was that my status changed from childless to father of three kids very quickly and from salaried to no assured income all at the same time. Initially this resulted in me lying awake at night sweating with worry wondering how I could possibly find the clients that would fuel the start-up of my new consultancy. Like most entrepreneurs, I quickly realized that lying awake at night worrying was not helping achieve my goals. Instead, relying on my faith and optimism (and exercise) I got a good night's sleep and woke early to work hard all day at business development. In no time, I was winning clients and earning more money than I had as an accountant. Many ask how I made this leap of faith.

Serial entrepreneurs with multiple start-ups under their belt know what behaviours lead to success. They also have failures that have taught them what not to do. In these cases, experience fuels their optimism but for me, despite having had businesses as a student I had never previously started a consultancy in Hong Kong.

Some entrepreneurs have grown up in a culture of success where everything they ever did ended up in a winning situation. In these cases, life experience is their source of optimism. These people may also have experienced failure but like most optimists (myself included) we believe even failures are successes because they teach you things you need to know.

There is another source of optimism which I call faith. Faith comes from belief but what you believe in may differ between people. For example, in religious contexts people gain their optimism from their belief in God or scripture. In the natural world people gain their optimism from nature's ability to renew itself through the cycle of life and birth (the seasons). In the achievement world people gain their optimism from the belief that hard work and sacrifice will pay off in the end. In the guru world people gain optimism believing in a guru, normally someone who has achieved greatness in a discipline and through example, coaching and helping others do the same. And finally, there are people who gain optimism from belief in their personal experience knowing that life is suffering, that they have overcome problems in the past and can do it again.

When the Great Recession wiped out many of my client's businesses, I witnessed senior people with normally assured jobs get fired and asked to relocate their families with only a week's notice. I remained optimistic through this knowing the recession was not my fault and that the best thing I could do was to show my children how to benefit from this adversity. At the time, I thought about my grandfather Frank Nixon whom I never knew because he died quite young, possibly due to the hardships he faced raising his young family in the Great Depression. I believed that if I cut my costs and focused on positive results I would come out of the Great Recession in a better place. Realising the volume of client work would suffer for some time I sat down to write my second book entitled *Dialogue Gap*. The book went on to great acclaim (SCMP "the best business title penned this century") and led to my being invited around the world to help leaders deal with problems highlighted in the book. I learned subsequently that most bestselling business books arise from recessions when the economy slows, and authors have time to reflect on their experience. This is another example of a positive outcome arising from a negative situation. Some say, "pressure makes diamonds", or "storms create rainbows". It is easy to say but only after you have lived through enough difficulties do you really accept that positive things will arise from negative situations. Experienced businesspeople will in fact search for opportunities in crisis. Faith that crisis brings opportunity is a source of optimism for experienced people.

Parenting experts remind us of the importance of enabling children to constantly push out their comfort zone. Yes, sometimes children will fail or hurt themselves but in doing so they will also build their confidence and belief in themselves. Later in life when facing the daunting situations life inevitably throws at us, children with more life experience will make it through the rough spots much more effectively than those who have been coddled and protected through life.

Not all people consider themselves optimists, some struggle to remain optimistic and some are natural pessimists. In Hong Kong, you do not need to look far to find people lacking in faith and optimism and turning instead to substance, retail therapy (shopping), or gambling abuse to sooth their challenges. Some fear the unknown more than the sad situations they live through daily (e.g. spousal abuse or a terrible employer) but lack the faith and bravery to make a change. What can we do to boost the faith and optimism needed to overcome the cultural hurdles standing between us and our development goals?

2013 was a test of my faith and optimism. My father and aunt both died. My wife hurt herself seriously on a hiking trip when she fell off a cliff and all three of my children were hospitalised for various sporting injuries. It was such a tough year that everyone expected something to happen to me. On top of that I also moved office that year and travelled further for business than any year of my life. When the year ended, I was glad to celebrate New Year's and turn the page to a fresh start and another year. What enabled me to keep my faith and remain optimistic through this difficult series of events? Teamwork is one thing that helped. My brothers, friends and hospital staff were there at every step along the way. The wider family gathered in support for my father and aunt and we held back to back funerals for them. My wife and I had experienced many sporting injuries with our kids so in some respects these were the easier events but my wife's fall was a game changer because she chose not to return to work and instead, after her rehabilitation, launched full time into the parenting consulting business which she began years before as a part-time business. Now she is principal at City Kids.

When everything crashes around you at the same time, I find these points to be immensely helpful.

1. One ingredient is accepting bad things happen and doing your best to enjoy the happy moments we are given when life is going well.
2. Another is being grateful for the service and care of the health professionals who are doing their best in difficult conditions to provide the best care they can often in emotionally challenging situations.
3. Another ingredient is accepting bad things happen but your reaction to these situations is what matters most. What I have learned about mindfulness, presence and compassion have been helpful watching fate ebb and flow in my life and in the lives of those close to me.
4. Another habit that helped me through the lows of 2013 and again now in the pandemic is my routine of work (when I am working with clients it is mostly impossible to think of other things)
5. And finally exercising regularly to tire my body and ensure a good night sleep even when suffering from jet lag seems to have served me well. Commonly my exercise includes walking amidst nature which also allows me to literally smell the flowers, play with puppies along the trail and share a laugh with others I meet along the way (all of whom are suffering through their own situations as well).

I have always sought out people that seemed to me to have figured out life better than most. This is what led me to spend time together with two famous monks, the 14th Dalai Lama and Thich Nhat Hahn. The former famously maintained his faith and optimism despite losing his country and watching his fellow countrymen suffer under Chinese Communist rule. The latter suffered through the French and American wars in Vietnam before fleeing to France and the USA to set up his Plum Village and bring peace to hundreds of thousands of followers. Interestingly both men are Buddhist and I believe their faith and optimism arose from their deep belief in suffering, emptiness, and compassion.

During my university years, I enjoyed the movie and music of *The Blues Brothers* which featured John Belushi and Dan Ackroyd. One of their famous lines was they were on a mission from God. Their story is a tale of redemption for paroled convict Jake and his brother Elwood, who set out on "a mission from God" to save from foreclosure the Catholic orphanage in which they were raised. To do so, they must reunite their R&B band and organize a performance to earn the $5,000 needed to pay the orphanage's property tax bill. In some countries as many as 85% of people say their source of faith arises from God. There is obvious debate about which God believers are referring to (depending on their religion) and the debate extends to atheists who do not believe there are any Gods whatsoever.

It is not my role here to argue the existence of God. I leave it to you the reader to decide your position on this question and I do not question your religious faith or lack thereof. What I do find especially important is that from your beliefs you can draw strength and from that strength optimism to gain the resilience necessary to overcome the challenges that are guaranteed in life. While we do not know, what challenges will befall us (or when) we do know that all of us will encounter problems eventually. Successful leaders prepare for these situations before they arrive while everyone else deal with life's offering (not always that well) as it comes along.

2013 was not the only challenging part of my life as an expatriate Canadian living abroad (expatriates and migrants understand the unique suffering caused by living away from your home and loved ones). As my wife and I worked to build our family we also suffered repeated miscarriages. Still to this day when I see an ultrasound, I remember the deep sadness the time I looked at the screen and realised for a third time that our foetus had stopped growing. How did we overcome these challenges which cause so many couples to split up? Part of our faith came from knowing many couples suffer similar problems. Part of our faith came from the fact we had always planned to adopt and instead of having a biological child first we could simply adopt first and then voila our beautiful daughter Ni Si arrived. Out of deep sadness came great joy. I am reminded from ancient India that we hold our hands together in prayer because it represents our wish that the person to whom you are praying will flower like the Lotus which grows out of the dark dirty mud under water into a beautiful flower above the surface shining in the sun. Our children, like many families, are the result of a great number of things happening that we could have never predicted. Miscarriages; babies being surrendered for adoption; matching panels connecting our kids with my wife and I as their adoptive parents; and the evolution of hormones making it possible for my wife to stay pregnant and have our own child (Jean-Pierre) and brother to our second adopted child Long Tim. These are all examples of having faith that things will work out for the best and to remain optimistic through all the challenges as they come your way. I do not want to leave you thinking it was all happiness going through these dark times. Sometimes loud music, a stiff drink, a good friend, or a walk outside are also useful antidotes for what life throws at us.

People who have achieved a lot in their careers tend to do what they love and love what they do. This synergy tends to attract others and the hours of alignment means they become recognized for their work and in time get paid more for doing it. In appearance, these people operate from a place of optimism and faith that others find inspiring but most of these people do things on a regular basis to maintain their faith and optimism. Here are just a few of those things:

1. **Daily focus** on things that bring them inspiration such as listening to music, looking at photos, walking in nature, prayer, meditation etc.

2. **Daily interaction** with positive people who bring sunshine into their lives including partners, children, friends, mentors, neighbours, parents, grandparents etc.
3. **Daily activities** to get themselves into the zone where challenge and accomplishment interact to provide satisfaction such as: sport, exercise, yoga, gardening, reading, writing, playing music, taking photos etc.
4. **Daily routines** to enhance health including good diet, sufficient sleep, minimal intact of alcohol, plenty of clean air, quiet times etc.
5. **Daily work they love** to realise their potential while helping others realise theirs

Organisations

Given that unprecedented change surrounds us we all want to work in positive organisations. Companies and institutions that have been around a long time tend to have more faith and optimism than start-ups which normally fail in less than two years. Companies that show the most resilience are those built on robust vision and mission. If your vision and mission take the long view (e.g. to provide premium accommodation to business travelers globally) then it is a lot easier to sustain success over long periods. If your vision and mission incorporate a deadline (e.g. to get a man to the moon and back before the end of the century) then you set your own limits.

Bankrupt companies are companies that mismanage their assets and liabilities blindly optimistic that sales and profitability will continue unabated. I think here of private gyms which typically sell a lot of memberships in bull markets but are also one of the first luxuries that people surrender in a bear market.

Bankrupt companies also include those that install blind faith into the future of their product or service. Think of the demise of bookstores, music shops and newspapers all of which may have faced their futures with optimism, but blind faith led them to bankruptcy.

Choosing to ignore financial hemorrhage or a drop in sales due to market changes seldom leads to success. Likewise, corporate leaders should not ignore personnel issues (e.g. stress, conflict, overwork) that can cause talent to pick up and leave to work for competitors with noticeably short notice. Be alert.

Usually when the end comes companies make it as fast and painless as possible. Following termination notices, I have seen senior executives escorted out of the premises, kids pulled from schools and families forced to move away with only a week's notice.

With a view to sustainability, effective dialogue, risk management, contingency planning, teamwork, compassion leave and support for victims of burnout are just some of the strategies successful organisations use when dealing with situations where faith and optimism are lacking.

One of the areas I enjoy in the schoolwork that I do is connecting with people focused on altruism, compassion, and positive psychology. In this regard, I have a lot of time for the work of Goldie Hawn, Martin Seligman and all those that have followed their lead in helping our young people develop resilience at a young age. My value for education came from both my father and mother. My father, despite an amazing memory for details, missed the chance to attend university when his father died of a heart attack while my father was serving in WWII. It also came from my mother who did attend McGill University obtaining a Science degree in Physical Education. In addition to my mother, my grandmother, wife, and daughter all graduated from education at McGill.

National

At the national level, there are lots of examples where the faith and optimism of leaders and citizens are tested. People who lived through the attack on the World Trade Center Towers in New York City will always remember Mayor Rudy Giuliani's ability to maintain faith and optimism as the emergency crews and victims dealt with the America's greatest attack on its home soil. Another example that now holds its place in history is British Prime Minister Sir Winston Churchill's rallying cry to the people of Britain during the darkest hours of World War Two. In both these situations the problems were overwhelming but both leaders knew that demonstrating deep faith and optimism was what their followers needed. If societal leaders admit defeat then their followers, with lesser perspective of the horizon, are sure to feel lost.

It is in the face of problems that a leader's faith and optimism are tested the most. "On your watch" is the leader's reality knowing anything can happen during your time as leader and what really counts is your ability to respond. At the heart of your response is your own faith and optimism.

Not all societal situations are confronted with faith and optimism. I joined his holiness the Dalai Lama for his Puja in Dharamshala to pray for the 100 monks and nuns that had chosen to self-immolate in protest of Chinese rule of Tibet. They had lost faith in the future and their actions, like suicides everywhere, caused more people to do the same. In Palestine I met several people that having spent generations in refugee camps had also lost faith and optimism that Israel would ever agree to grant them freedom. Violence, they believed, was the only option. Sometimes blind faith can overrule reality as it did in the Iraq War where the invasion proceeded on an assumption of weapons of mass destruction hidden in the sand when in fact no weapons were ever found to exist.

Solutions

I sometimes feel the more I travel and witness the state of the world today the more I resist the impact of PTSD (post-traumatic stress disorder) because the moment you leave the shelter of your world (assuming you come from a stable home and community) you begin seeing the problems we have created and face together in the world. At the same time however, you meet beautiful people all working in their own ways to make the world a better place. I choose to hang my hat with those who have faith and toil to make the world a better place, optimistic that if I help even a few people I will have not lived in vain. In the pandemic we can think of the front-line workers who give it their all so the rest of us can carry on some semblance of normality in our lives.

Despite the interest caused by this pandemic, organised religion needs to do a serious brand audit because globalization and the internet have combined to speed up the haemorrhage of believers in their ranks. At the same time the world today is looking for connections more than ever before so while religious beliefs might need some refining the caring community created by organized religion is something to be developed (provided religions are open to each other and don't argue their religion is better than others). In most countries, most schools and hospitals are still operated by (or were founded by) religious organisations. In this regard, I am delighted to work with McGill University's School of Religious Studies and the Tony Blair Faith Foundation which are exploring ways to integrate religious understanding into medicine, law, education, science, and business.

At the end of the day, farmers since the beginning of time, like my ancestors did when they emigrated to Canada, (see about author) have sown seeds in faith and optimism that after the growing season they would harvest life sustaining food. While this is not always the case, if floods, droughts, insects, and fires intervene, one thing they know for sure is that if you do not plant seeds you will not harvest any results. Be like farmers who plant seeds, have faith, remain optimistic when things go wrong and then with persistence at the right time harvest what they sow and more.

What can leaders, companies and nations do to develop their faith and optimism without falling victim of blind faith?

1. Leaders should take part in the daily activities listed above to develop their faith and optimism

2. Companies should periodically test the assumptions behind their vision and mission and engage in dialogue with people holding opposing views. When questions arise effective risk management and contingency planning should be discussed.

3. Nations should select leaders with demonstrated faith, optimism and resilience and ensure proper crisis management plans are in place for problems when they arise be, they natural or man-made.

Potentialism

The world needs a new direction

I have worked in most major economies in the world and can safely say the battle between capitalism and communism has not achieved optimal outcomes for most species on earth, we humans included. Mass migrations, the concentration of capital in the richest 1%, the conversion of wealth into intangible assets like big data, brands, and intellectual capital, rampant materialism, alienation of people connected by the internet but unable to talk to each other in person, plastic oceans, climate change, and pandemics are but a few of the problems we face today. We need a new direction.

The new direction, as always is being pointed out by young people around the world. The sharing economy is a result of people no longer being able to buy their own home, car or even bike. What is the use of individual ownership when people can share? Unfortunately, the internet has prevented the natural progression towards social democracy by creating echo chambers where people mostly listen to opinions which match their own.

The 21st century needs to be based on a system that promotes dialogue between the polarised groups, a system that can incorporate the best of capitalism and socialism without getting bogged down in the problems of each. The dialogue that is needed must be civil and supported by leaders who are themselves prepared to listen to opposing views and change their beliefs when a better way can be found.

Optimal outcomes cannot be achieved by ideologues who believe exclusively in their ideas and demonise opponents. Regimes that criminalise opponents and silence dissent will never enable the dialogue needed to change when required to continue to achieve optimal outcomes. Systems that cannot change in step with the ever-changing realities of their populace are doomed to failure. Only systems that promote dialogue and resolve conflict between stakeholders, no matter how hard this is, will achieve optimal outcomes over time.

Capitalism's unhinged greed has led to deadly pollution, wealth gaps and social strife around the world. Since most people lose out in a pure capitalist system (a few get rich while jobs migrate to the poorest countries), it is inevitable that poor people (the majority) will always search for an economic alternative to capitalism.

Karl Marx's 1867 *Das Kapital* (Marxism) became the solution for people seeking a remedy for capitalism. Politicians recognising the popularity of Marxism jumped on the band wagon could get themselves elected. In some countries, once elected, the communists made sure they remained in power forever leading to a litany of complaints by the people like what originally drove them away from capitalism.

Communism has flourished in the Eastern Bloc, South East Asia, Africa, and Latin American countries but after several decades it has proven to be less efficient than capitalism at creating wealth for its citizens. The rich became richer in capitalist countries and the poor remained poorer in the socialist countries. By the time of the collapse of the Soviet Union in 1989, capitalism was considered to have won the 20th century battle between prevailing economic theories but perceived success didn't last long before the ills of capitalism were again exposed by the Genie Index and Occupy Movements exposing excessive wealth gaps around the world.

As cracks appears in the market economics the next response by world leaders was to reinforce the system through multilateral agreements, innovative dialogue at Davos, and police crackdown on dissent around the world.

In China paramount leader Deng Xiaoping suggested "socialism does not mean shared poverty" and instituted economic reforms to harness the market economy calling it "socialism with Chinese characteristics". These changes coupled with the rapid growth in international trade led to the shareholders in the West getting richer as profits improved by moving manufacturing to lower cost countries like China. Workers in China also got rich during this era of unprecedented growth in the global economy but two groups were being overlooked. As the world got richer, two groups, the unemployed blue collar workers in the West who lost their jobs to factories in China and unemployed white collar workers and youth globally whose traditional jobs were being replaced by computerisation and elimination of inefficiencies on a local or national level.

Another age-old problem became apparent as the systems began to fall apart. People did all they could to enrich themselves before the system collapsed. In companies leaders paid themselves huge bonuses even when share prices were collapsing and people were being made redundant. In government bureaucrats were being caught in corrupt practices made easier through market influences.

Whether you emphasise making profits (Capitalism), eliminating the class divide (socialism), or maintaining party control (Communism), none of these 20th century systems have led to optimal outcomes. We need new language to eliminate debate about the other. We need an economic system that puts achieving potential as the heart of policy and promotes dialogue to find and achieve optimal outcomes amongst the stakeholders. We need to treat all species and our environment as stakeholders. We need to build on the diversity of humanity, not claim one group is better than another.

After studying this problem for several decades, I propose *Potentialism* as the solution we need for the 21st century. Based on effective dialogue between individual and collective rights, potentialism harnesses the power of human greed while meeting the needs of the stakeholders and protecting the environment in which we live.

What is Potentialism?

Potentialism is the belief that "we have a duty to realise our potential while helping others realise theirs". This continuous dialogue between personal and collective interests is underpinned by the 1994 Nobel Prize winning economics of mathematician John Nash, made famous in the 2001 Ron Howard film *A Beautiful Mind*.

Nash's *Governing Dynamics Theory* is an upgrade on Adam Smith's *Invisible Hand Theory*, coined by Smith in his 1776 book *The Wealth of Nations*. Smith, who is considered the father of economics, suggested that individual self-interest when sought after would at the same time benefit the economy by generating wealth for others.

Adam Smith's theory has been held up ever since as an excuse to minimise the role of government in the economy but Nash proved that only when the equilibrium point between self-interest and the interests of others is found, can an economy be optimised.

In simple terms, *Nash's Equilibrium* is the point at which no one party can gain more without other parties losing something. It is the point at which everyone has the best deal possible at the time. I call this point the *optimal outcome* and my work in negotiation, dialogue and business development has always aimed at helping clients achieve this point, however elusive due to conflict, incomplete information, or lack of skill. I represent the optimal outcome as a jewel in all of my graphics because the optimal outcome will be different in different situations based on the elements of the dialogue situation (stakeholders, issues, time, space, way it is achieved).

What does Potentialism mean in practical terms?

Potentialism requires dialogue between stakeholders to find what is best for each party. The dialogue gap which presently exists between our need for dialogue and our leaders ability and willingness to engage in dialogue is the cause of our problems today.

To overcome our current problems, we need to train and encourage our leaders to dialogue with the key stakeholders involved in achieving an optimal outcome. In the 21st century we are no longer playing a zero-sum game of winners and losers. As the pandemic has reminded us, if one person is sick somewhere, everyone is sick everywhere. If the economy of one country collapses, millions of citizens migrate to other countries to improve their chances of survival thereby hurting the economy of the receiving country. If Asia is left to pollute their continent, environmentalism in the West is insufficient to save the climate. In the 21st century we must be our brother's keeper because like it or not, we all live in the same house, the 3rd planet from the sun. And on top of all the problems we have living together in that house, our house itself is struggling with climate change.

Since potentialism means "we have a duty to realise our potential while helping others realise theirs", this dialogue can be stimulated by asking a simple question:

"How might we achieve an optimal outcome for all species while protecting the environment in which we live"?

In the situations below, the hottest topics we face today, I apply *Potentialism* to test this economic theory and see what we need to do differently as a result.

Potentialism Applied

Concern Areas	Individual Rights	Collective Rights	Environmental Rights
Housing	People should feel the desire to work and buy a better house	Government should provide free housing of a minimum standard for the homeless	Home construction (materials and location) should respect the environment
Health	People can work to enjoy better healthcare	Minimum healthcare should be free	Healthcare products and practices should respect the environment
Freedom of speech	People have the right to express themselves	Inciting hate and criminal activity not allowed	Advocates must speak on behalf of the environment
Democracy	People should have the right to vote and choose their leaders	Political parties should ensure social and economic stability	Government must protect the environment on behalf of all
Education	People should be allowed to buy a private education if they want	Children should be entitled to a free quality public K-13 education	Education about protecting the environment should be part of the curriculum
Migration	People should be allowed to apply to migrate to better countries	Governments should work to keep all their citizens happy so they don't want to leave	Governments must partner with others when natural disasters necessitate migration
Policing	People should be able to trust their police and protest peacefully	Police should dialogue and not escalate use of force for political means	Governments should police environment as well as people and assets
Pollution	People should be able to produce goods and services while pollution free	Government should punish individuals and companies that pollute	Production of goods and services should not externalise costs at the expense of environment
International Trade	People should be free to buy anything from anywhere	Countries should produce onshore if at all possible	Goods and services must include the environmental cost of global trade
Corruption	Self-interest is the engine of capitalism but honesty and integrity should be promoted and exemplified by leaders	Leaders taking undue advantage or engaging in corrupt practices should be exposed and removed	Those responsible for damaging our environment through corrupt practices should be heavily sentenced
Materialism	Consumers should be entitled to purchase what they want	Governments should dissuade people from accumulation of stuff	Recycling, reduce, re-use should be enforced everywhere
Media	People should be allowed to watch and listen to what they	Media should be monitored to eliminate fake news, hate speech	All media should be responsible for some content promoting and protecting the

	want	etc	environment

Pensions	People should be able to save for a richer retirement	A minimum living wage should be provided for pensioners and unemployed	Pensioners should be required to clean up the environment to receive monthly support
Taxation	Individuals should be able to spend their tax dollars where they want	Government should tax all profits 20% and manage where people spend their contribution	Governments should have a list for private taxpayers to support environmental projects in their own name
Entrepreneurship	Everyone should give entrepreneurship a try at some point	Schools, colleges, and universities should all teach entrepreneurship	Government should help direct entrepreneurial investments into environmental protection
Banking	All profits should be taxed 20% regardless of on or offshore	Global supervision is needed to track currency flows	Offshore financial centres should be given alternative sources to make money if their banking is brought back to where money is made
Unions	People should be allowed to unionise	Unions have to partner with business to achieve an optimal outcome	Unions need to consider the environmental impact of their decisions too
Military Defence	Individual right to bear arms is not to create a military insurrection	Military should be created for defence and natural disaster response	Military should be used across borders to protect the environment

How to spread the word

Capitalism, communism, socialism, and environmentalism all started with an idea and spread globally as people shared their inspiration for a better future. It is envisaged potentialism will be no different. In fact, some are already talking about setting up *The Potential Party* in their country. I do not see myself becoming a legislator in Canada (where I am a citizen) or in Hong Kong (where I presently reside). Instead I see my role as advising leaders who want to put potentialism at the heart of their policy making in their country.

The post pandemic world will never be about making one country great again at the expense of another. The post pandemic world will be about working together to achieve an optimal outcome for all stakeholders. The pandemic reminded us that if anyone is sick anywhere, everyone is sick everywhere. In this new era a new approach is required. As climate change and coronavirus remind us, we 7 billion are in this together and local, state, and national policies must "help realise our potential while helping others realise theirs".

Conclusion

"Once the fruit is plucked from the tree of knowledge,
the way back to Eden is barred forever." (Csikszentmihalyi)

Focusing upon the achievement of optimal outcomes to develop leaders and nations might sound like an endorsement of capitalist theory. Having grown up during the cold war and watched the evolution of the Soviet Union, China, Vietnam and other socialist countries successfully switch from central planning to market based economies, it is clear the market system does a better job harnessing human motivation thereby benefiting individuals and collective interests.

Despite acknowledging the supremacy of market forces, I do not recommend uncontrolled capitalism because it leads to problems we want to avoid. Instead of pure capitalism I side with John Nash who proved what is good for the markets is what is good for the individual AND the other party. This is the basis of my work in dialogue, negotiation, and development. If you want to get the optimal outcome you need to focus on the needs of the other party as well. The growing gap between rich and poor and the rapidly diminishing prospects for our environment are proof enough that selfishness is not the way ahead should we all (7 billion and counting) want to live successfully together on planet earth. Likewise, as we can see with the crackdown on free speech in Hong Kong, communism also is a failed system because if excludes dialogue leading to self-improvement.

I conclude this book with the following suggestions for leaders who want to improve their organisations and nations:
- know and be themselves
- focus and stay on course
- allow for change and change for good
- develop your mind, body, and spirit
- jump the hurdles

Know & Be Yourself

How does an accountant in Montreal become an international speaker, author and expert negotiator based in Hong Kong and working around the world? The simple answer is "one step at a time". The longer answer was outlined in this book. Like many people whose career twists and turns through time and space, mine was no exception. Of course if you told me when I was working in Montreal in the 1980's that I'd raise my family in Hong Kong, publish bestselling books and speak in 60 countries I'd have thought you were crazy and would have probably told you so, insulting you and proving myself wrong at the same time.

Through my work I have been privileged to meet a lot of amazing leaders. Almost all of them told me that as teenagers they would have never anticipated being where they are today. But there is some commonality amongst people surprised by their success because most earned their success so if you are wondering what small change can bring a big return in your career the anecdotes in this book have been captured and shared for you.

This book is intended to serve as your career Lonely Planet Guide, full of tips from people who have journeyed before you and given me the chance to share their stories thereby enabling your journey to be more successful and less frightening.

I knew a bit about myself when I went away to college but like most young adults in those formative years, I learned a LOT more about myself in a short amount of time. Moving away from the shelter, guidance and expectations of parents is for most people one of the most traumatic and yet enriching period of their lives. This is true whether it happens at 14 when you are sent to boarding school, 18 when you go to college or years later when you move in with a partner for the first time, or lose your parents one way or another.

When you still live with your parents you typically find yourself role-playing either as child, grandchild, brother, sister etc. However, when you move out you get to know yourself better and find that some of these roles fit, some of the roles drive you crazy and other roles fall somewhere in the middle.

In getting to know yourself you need an understanding of your likes and dislikes, dreams & fears, skills, blind spots, and weaknesses. Having the chance to complete style assessments such as the Strength Deployment Inventory (Scudder), MBTI (Myers-Briggs) and others is a great way to know more about yourself. Likewise, performance feedback, appraisals, 360-degree feedback and coaching are also great ways to learn more about your strengths and weaknesses.

It is also important to understand how you fit into the world, your family, your neighbourhood, your nation, and the world. To learn about these topics, I recommend being a reflective practitioner which means do not just work all the time, periodically take a time out to reflect on your practice. Identify what went well and what can be improved. Collect feedback. Jump hurdles – challenge yourself and others for continuous improvement.

Finally, you also need to understand how you are affected by your culture and how your culture fits together with other cultures in the world. In this regard, it is useful to consider the cultural hurdles assessment offered in the appendix and discuss the results with your colleagues.

When I was a boy the first image of the earth was taken from outer space and it began changing peoples' minds forever. *Earthrise*, the 1968 photo taken by Apollo 8 astronaut William Anders is considered one of the most influential environmental photographs every taken. For the first time we had a perspective of our whole world given to us from beyond our world. This photograph gave us both a finite and collective view of the world. After centuries exploring our world on earth, we could finally see the whole world in one photograph and accept that was all there was. It helped us realise that we will make or break our existence on this little planet and that there are no more brave new worlds to conquer and exploit (although we learn more about outer space and ocean floors every day).

About the same time this image of the earth appeared my parents bought our family a copy of the *World Book Encyclopaedia* and for the first time we could see all the world's knowledge in one place. Encyclopaedias helped define what we knew and what we did not. I set about reading every book in the collection, each topic divided by letter. I soon realised it was a daunting task to read, remember and make sense of all the knowledge contained in the World Book. About the same time Architect Buckminster Fuller's geodesic dome *Spaceship Earth* was built for the US Pavilion at the 1967 world exhibition in Montreal. This impressive structure remains today as a legacy of Expo '67. At that point in history it was impressive to see what I thought to be the whole world coming together in my hometown. What we needed to know then but largely ignored and still overlook today was Buckminster Fuller's book *Operating Manual for Spaceship Earth*. This would have reminded us about some of the limits to the environment which are now behind us. About the same time EF Schumacher's ground breaking book, *Small is Beautiful*, gave us yet another perspective of our world and an early reminder of the unstainable nature of our human existence in the world then.

The world carried on into the 1970's and 80's during which we resolved the Cold War, nations gained independence and globalisation resumed its march through our civilisations. The 1990's and 2000's topped off world economic development with international trade growing at the fastest pace in a century, emerging markets created billionaires and we began resolving various health and environmental issues. Now however, as we approach the 2020's, climate change, species collapse, unprecedented wealth gap, human migration, and the finite nature of our world, first brought to our attention in the 1960's, are all streaming on our smart phones and motivating us to retreat and build walls.

The state of the world is motivating people in different ways. Some people, including a lot of the rich and lucky in the world, look at the situation and do all they can to amass and protect wealth knowing their luck might well run out sooner rather than later. A second group of people, coming from a wide variety of backgrounds and economic standing, toil away to create a more sustainable world. A third group carry on as before resigned to the fact they cannot or do not want to influence change. After all what can one person do to effect change in a world of seven billion people?

Well that is exactly the point. YOU do make a difference. As Chaos Theory reminds us, if a butterfly flaps its wings, it can impact weather patterns in another part of the world. We are all in this together. If you go back far enough in time, we are all related to each other. It is only due to history that we think we can ignore people and problems "over there" thinking they will not affect us personally. The world now lives together, in one village, with different cultures and languages brushing up against each other on an hourly basis. We need dialogue to live together productively and address the global concerns affecting each one of us regardless of where we live.

Does the world know itself? Research by NASA, leading universities and data collected by satellites, drones, and the internet, is helping us better understand the state of the world today. We know who consumes, who produces, who invents and who copies others. We know health statistics, religious affiliations, war zones, terrorist ideology, child mortality and economic indicators. We know who is corrupt, who lobbies whom and who censors information we want to share. We know who controls our resources, media, and military. Now that we know pretty much everything what is the world doing with this awareness?

The world is moving forward according to the trends of the people that make it up. While some parts of the world are getting better, others are getting worse. Overall, if you believe the environmental scientists, we collectively are not doing well at all. So, what to do? One thing the world should do is be itself. If every nation begins acting, dressing, and consuming like the media dominant Western Nations then we risk losing our cultural diversity and vibrancy and consumption rates will doom our planet. If on the other hand, we carry on as we are now, we will never solve the underlying sustainability issues we face globally.

"Life provides both our barometer of progress and our final exam." (Goleman)

Jump the hurdles

I have been jumping hurdles my whole life. When I was young, I realised if I simply worked a few jobs after school I could join other local and international Boy Scouts at the World Jamboree in Norway. A few years later I realised if I worked and studied at the same time I could save up and go away to college. It seems I have been working hard ever since, not happy with my lot in life and preferring to experience more, travel farther, learn more, speak to more people, try different jobs etc. In a strange twist of fate, it was probably my adventurous and inquisitive nature that has taken me millions of miles around the world only to leave me content finally to stay home exactly where I began.

One thing I have learned is that people who want to be leaders and leaders who want to be successful will need to be constantly pushing the envelope, biting off more than they can chew, because in doing so you will learn new things, conceptualise new ideas, understand different perspectives and fuel your motivations for better than before. The world needs leaders wanting to take on the big problems we are facing and the leaders that are given the chance to contribute their talents will be those who demonstrate their willingness and track record in pushing the envelope.

I encourage you to be constantly widening your comfort zone. If there is something you have not done, try it. If there is a core skill you are not good at, try to learn it. If there is information critical to your success, go find it. Talk to the people you would normally be embarrassed to talk to. Be brave, go for it. It is only in trying new things that you will find what you like and do not like and what you are good at or not. Careers keep changing with jobs being invented while others falling into history. The same is true with your skills so you want to pick up all the skills you can when you are young and keep learning throughout your lifetime.

The United Nations and similar multi-lateral organisations are leading the way in helping promote engagement and dialogue amongst world leaders. The more we promote the use of the internet, face to face interaction and education to bring people together on the issues that matter, the better will be our efforts to act in unison to solve the challenges facing our world.

In joining arms, we need to remember the elements of effective dialogue (presence, respect, expression, suspending and absorbing) and create the space needed for changes in thinking, innovation, and breakthrough ideas to be realised. Great work is already being done in this regard through exchanges (e.g. Kids4Peace), site visits (e.g. Leaders Quest) and education (e.g. Face to Faith) but we must do more and put dialogue skills training into schools, universities and corporate curriculums globally.

When dialogue is effective it begins to melt away the conceptions arising from ignorance and avoidance. Beliefs such as I am right and you are wrong; there is only one way to do things; we can't do better and other limiting views of the world must evolve into a willingness to try new ways of doing things; an openness and acceptance of other ways of being and a realisation that sharing is better than continuing our have vs. have not paradigm.

Nations must jump hurdles in terms of economy, infrastructure, healthcare, education, environment, and social harmony knowing failure to do so will cause them to fall behind the community of world leading nations.

Focus & Stay on Course

I guarantee you will fail, face frustration, get depressed, think the world is against you and want to turn back through fear, burnout or being side-tracked by other pursuits you find along your journey that seem more enticing. It is ESPECIALLY important that you not build your career like a weathervane, changing course as the wind blows. If you really want to succeed you need to set your direction and stick to it. Check your compass or GPS from time to time and ensure you keep on track. It is ok if you decide to change your desired destination but it is not ok for you to waste time and effort going off track when in pursuit of your goals.

To keep your course, you will need to learn to control your emotions to enhance your situation rather than hinder it. Practice the emotion control tactics outlined in the appendix. Recognise the negative emotions that can and will divert your focus just when you need it most. My father's uncle George Ewing, who was Mayor of Melbourne Quebec and owner of his own successful furniture business on the St Francis River, stepped into mentor my father after he lost his own father from heart attack. George Ewing used to tell everyone who knew him that "You can't manage others until you can manage yourself". What he was referring to, was that successful leaders need to stay focused even as the winds change. Leaders interested in identifying more about the negative impact of their leadership behaviours should read Professor Robin Stuart-Kotze's book *Performance* (FT Pearson, 2006) to assess their negative behaviours when compared to other leaders.

It is natural for all of us to be challenged and fall off course or slow-down from time to time. The key is to know how you are doing and constantly recalibrate to remain on your course and achieving your goals without wallowing in the wind or pursuing goals and dreams that are not you own. You have only one life, be sure to live your life and not someone else's.

The road ahead for the world is not getting any easier and we need our leaders to overcome the hurdles and meet the challenge. Since we do not want mutual self-destruction, we need to realise our potential while helping other nations realise theirs. We need to help mentor failing states toward better governance because our success is measured by the least successful amongst us and we cannot progress if we leave people behind. We need to protect human rights while respecting human rights as well. Leaders that limit the success of some groups, while promoting personal and success and wealth, are not contributing to national success. Tyrants in one country create havoc for all countries. To prevent this, we need to better develop and choose our leaders. To keep focus and direction we need more opportunities for engagement and dialogue amongst world leaders, not just at the top of government and multinational corporations but also amongst people at lower levels in public, private and charity sectors as well.

Like multi-national companies moving regularly across borders, countries to need to share best practices and keep each other up to date because those who fall behind will also be losing jobs to competing markets. If some countries fall too far behind e.g. Syria, the people from these failed states will flood the successful states thereby slowing them down as well.

> [Stanford University historian Ian Morris] "sees our ability
> to evolve culturally as the capacity that lets us live in bigger,
> more interconnected societies than ever and keep the peace.
> The historian of war concludes,
> "The age-old dream of a world without war may yet come to pass." (Goleman)

Allow for change & Change for Good

Given the gap between rich and poor, now greater than at any time in history, it is natural to think everyone has only one goal in life which is to get rich. Some would say you need only look to the multitude of examples of corruption and greed made famous by the most prominent of society in countries around the world, to prove that wealth and not potential, is what drives people today.

I beg to differ. I believe most people in the world today march to the drum of a different drummer and rather than chase wealth, they instead aspire to make a positive difference at home, at work and in society. It appears that those who succeed most in their careers are not those that made money their goal but rather those who made to make a difference in serving others their goal. Entrepreneurs that launch the most successful products and services are those whose inventions help people the most. You never discover breakthrough ideas looking for money. Like the elusive Holy Grail, you may find you get close to success by chasing money but you will never find ultimate success by focusing on money over service to others.

To truly succeed you need to focus on helping people and to do so you must first look after yourself. Like a pregnant woman eating right and exercising regularly during her pregnancy so that her baby has the healthiest start in life possible, if we want to realise our potential and make a positive difference we need to develop our mind, body, and spirit.

You need only look at the daily headlines of leaders that either succeed or fail to see defining differences in how they lead their lives. A current analogy reminds us that while computers look similar, they certainly do not all operate in similar ways. Operating systems make a huge difference in computers and the same is true with humans. When leaders fail, it is as if they were missing an upgrade or patch for their operating software, controlling their mind, body, or spirit.

As I fly around the world to work with groups of people in governments, business, and charity groups, I meet people who are depressed and resigned to a sad future. I do not share this depressed view of the future but I do not deny it either. My view is fuelled by hope and faith that in our short time here on earth we can make the world a better place. The more we rise in our organisations or government the more significant our influence on the outcome of the future. If a sufficient percentage of leaders work together with hope and faith for a brighter future, we can realise our potential while helping others realise theirs and we will indeed have a brighter future.

A brighter future includes embracing change and helping people who are leading change, managing change or who are victims of change. Leaders should not allow for change to turn negative. Falling into a cycle of conflict and selfishness should never be the strategy for a nation. While fear might easily secure votes from those who are nervous about change, national leaders should be inspiring their populations to a brighter future and higher ideals, not pulling them in the opposite direction.

Develop your Mind, Body, & Spirit

Mind
In terms of developing your mind there is a lot of focus, especially in Asia, on getting into the "best" school. In fact, some people are so concerned with climbing the ladder they register foetuses at the "best" kindergarten to ensure they get their child into the best primary school so he or she can get into the "best" secondary school to get into the "best" university and graduate with an offer from the "best" employer working in the "best" nation. Unfortunately, development is not so simply.

The rising wealth of emerging nations has caused applications for leading universities to skyrocket making admission requirements harder and harder to attain and allowing for the cost of education to skyrocket along with demand. With all the world's information now available on the internet and some of the most famous universities offering free massive on-line open courses ("MOOC's"), what is the need to join the queue to get into the "best" university?

Instead of getting into the "best" whatever, people should instead be focused on realising their potential while helping other people realise theirs. What is the secret to realising your potential? People need to focus on all three elements, mind, body, and spirit, continuously throughout their lives. Overemphasising one of these three at any stage of your career will also causes problems.

Body

The fact we are getting increasingly obese due to our sedentary lifestyles and poor food selection is causing us all problems. As children, we learn a lot while playing physically with others and in doing so we burn calories and learn skills that help us later in life. In school the students that maintain routine exercise and sports benefit from reduced stress, increased ability to focus mentally and the chance to make friends and have fun engaging with others. Once we join the workforce a lot of us significantly reduce the amount of time spent exercising. Over the course of your career if you don't find ways to maintain an active lifestyle in your 20's, 30's and 40's then you will be facing serious problems with your physical and mental health heading into middle age. Once you are into your 50's the aches and pains of current and past injuries remind you daily of the need to step up your exercise. You also notice that the people who are in the best condition in their 60's, 70's, 80's and even 90's are those people who have maintained a healthy lifestyle (diet and exercise) on a regular basis throughout the years. Sadly, those who do not will unfortunately succumb to cancer or other sad illnesses leading to early death.

So, what must we do? Learn sports, get active, measure your daily exercise (there are many apps and devices now available) and keep at it without excuse daily. Eat and drink right and avoid drugs to create a healthy environment your mind, body, and spirit.

Spirit

By the time, I was seventeen, having already tasted the excitement of international travel two years earlier, I was eager to leave my parent's house so I enrolled at Champlain Regional College in Lennoxville. I spent the first few months living at King's Hall in Compton, a beautiful rural setting occupying the grounds of the former Compton School for Girls. Although the surroundings were good for the spirit the travel was not convenient so I applied to move into Norton Hall on campus, conveniently shared with Bishop's University where I studied after completing two years at Champlain.

While living at Norton Hall my father posted me a brief note, something he did weekly as a way of staying in touch before the advent of the internet and the drop in the cost of long-distance telephone calls. One of his notes resonated with me in a big way and I taped it to my mirror so I could see it all the time. I shared a room that year with Brooke McSkimming and I wonder if he remembers that note. It has gone onto influence my life ever since. It said:

> "You want to succeed and you will
> Manage talent, training, time, money, energy and people
> Most important of all
> Learn to control your emotions
> to enhance your situation rather than hinder it"

You will remember the challenge of controlling your emotions as a teenager and when you compound this with the freedom of living on a university campus at age 17 then you can imagine some of the challenges I was facing at the time.

I have spent the years ever since trying to figure out how to manage my emotions to enhance my situation rather than hinder it. I offer forty solutions in the appendix all of which I have found in my travels since that fateful year in Lennoxville.

I share this story because leaders need to nurture their spirit daily. Only by tending to their spirit daily can they remain present and unperturbed in the face of crisis and destructive emotions which are part of our human existence. Another benefit in doing so will be to garner compassion for their fellow employees, suppliers, customers, and bosses all of whom are suffering in their own way with the trials and tribulations life offers.

I was not very compassionate in the first half of my career, trained as I was to get ahead of others in class, compete with classmates for the best jobs and compete with colleagues for promotion. Professionally, as an auditor with one of the leading audit firms in the world, I was trained to search out both mistaken and intentional misstatements in the financial statements of the companies we were auditing. Since the profession values accuracy and completeness, finding fault in others work was praised. Unfortunately, I developed an attitude of competition rather than compassion. Later in my career as I explored destructive emotions in relation with negotiation and achieving optimal outcomes, I came to realise the folly of my ways. We can still climb to the stars without denigrating those around us. Everyone is striving to be happier and eliminate suffering. The last thing people need is for winners to remind them of their shortcomings.

I offer my research into the cultural hurdles separating winners and losers in a spirit of helping everyone succeed not to fault those who fall short of the finish line. Careers are not a zero-sum game. We can all succeed if we want to. The spirit of this book and hopefully your spirit as a leader reading it is one of compassion for the people, organisations, and nations that stumble trying to achieve their goals. As leaders, we should work to help others overcome these hurdles not shame them for their failures.

Develop Mind Body and Spirit – as a nation

When we think of mind, body, and spirit we are normally thinking of individuals. Nations are simply the collection of millions of individuals and when you think of it this way you can also begin to look at generalities. The mind, body and spirit of a nation tends to reflect the thought leaders most covered in the nation's media.

Mind

Think of your nation, what do you think people mostly think about? Are they focused on learning and developing their minds to better realise their potential or are they fritting away their attention on relatively thoughtless activities seeking pleasure or avoidance of work and other less pleasant tasks? When I was working in Chennai a few years ago I left the Taj where I was happily holed up and went for a walk to look around. I noticed the busiest spot near the hotel was the local bookshop where Indians of all ages, students, office workers, labourers, were lined up in the three-story bookshop by the hundreds reading, selecting, and purchasing books. Many of the world's bestsellers had been locally printed to make them as inexpensive and easily accessible to the common man as possible.

Frequent travellers are always struck by contrasts and my vision of the Chennai bookshop was still with me when I landed in China where I experienced glitzy shopping malls filled with the latest fashions and premium products but no bookshops. Computer game zones however were terribly busy.

It is perhaps unfair to compare India and China in this way but nonetheless is was my impression at the time and it seems to hold true in my work. In most parts of Asia including China I will assume none of my participants will have read the material but in India, as has happened on more than one occasion, the participants tell me when I arrive that they have already read everything including my books and wonder if there is anything more they can read before we begin.

The only point I wish to make is to ask you to reflect on your nation and whether thought leaders can direct the collective mind towards more productive thoughts. Setting a good example is the best way to do this. As wise people have said over the centuries, what you think is what you become.

Body
The world is suffering though a self-inflicted obesity crisis and some parts of the world are also suffering through substance abuse, over work, over stress and too much pollution. National leaders need to step up the focus on ensuring average people in their country are fit and through healthy diet and exercise, maintain healthy bodies through their lives. Doing so will not only lead to greater productivity as a nation, it will also lead to greater happiness and reduced healthcare costs. Jumping the hurdles described in this book requires fitness.

National thought leaders should also focus their attention on the infrastructure and environment of their nation's cities. While rural areas have mostly maintained their beauty (unless stripped of their natural resources and left barren), urban centres are today sometimes contributing to awful bodily experiences for their residents.   Traffic, pollution, lack of green spaces, unsafe neighbourhoods and a simple lack of common areas are all leading to less than optimal minds and bodies. We can and should do better.

Spirit
It is fitting to finish this book talking about our collective spirit. Individually we need to tend to our own personal spirit but collectively we also have a spirit. The world has been facing its biggest human migrations since WWII. Some nations have reacted by putting up walls while others have welcomed millions onto their lands. In nations and companies, we cannot separate ourselves from the headlines when our leaders are found guilty of corruption or worse. We glow in the sunlight when our leaders are respected locally or internationally for their integrity, creativity, or positive results.

National leaders need to take a long hard look at their people and their collective spirit. If their peoples are not realising their potential while helping others realise theirs then something is wrong. If they are depressed, quitting, migrating, protesting because they feel ignored, involved in crime or filling their days and nights with unhealthy diversions then you must work to improve the collective spirits of your people.

Corporate Social Responsibility (CSR) is leading many companies to harness the collective spirit of their workforce in a positive way. International development banks and the International Monetary Fund are helping developing nations build infrastructure, schools, hospitals and most importantly hope in people that have felt left behind by the world's progress.

Importantly we can never rest on our laurels because the world keeps spinning and as it does things change. We need to remember to keep focus on our collective mind, body and spirit while overcoming the cultural hurdles separating the winners from the losers.

If we meet along the way lets help each other out. It is our duty to realise our potential while helping others realise theirs. Pay it forward if you wish because in all religions we are reminded that doing so will lead to a more positive future and if you are not religious or think religion is responsible for a lot of the world's problems then think of it instead as faith and optimism. Lending a hand to others and helping them succeed, without any regard to repayment for your kindness, will boost their faith and optimism in humanity and in doing so we will all be better off.

I have two sayings that people who know me well have heard me say for years: *The solution is in the dialogue* and *the goal in life is to create happy memories*. If we should meet let's take a moment to engage in dialogue and talk about the happy memories we are creating for the people around us, be they family, friends, neighbours, work colleagues, fellow citizens or strangers from other parts of the world we have yet to befriend.

Jump the hurdles

Finally, these tips for jumping hurdles (from www.wikihow.com/hurdle) seem equally relevant to succeeding in the 2020's, to realise our potential while helping others realise theirs:
1. Stretch
2. Practice
3. Counts your steps
4. Sprint
5. Do not slow at the first hurdle
6. Drag the trail leg sideways over the side of the hurdle after the lead led has passed over
7. Continue the race and speed up at the end

Namaste,

Peter Nixon
Discovery Bay
Hong Kong

Appendix 1

INSPIRED	Unmotivated	Invigorating
	Bureaucratic	Enthusiastic
	Misdirected	Aligned

SUSTAIN	Short term	Honest
	Corrupt	Future Focus
	Self focus	Transparent

TRUSTEE	Selfish	Builder
	Uncaring	Protectors
	Egotistical	Legacy

OPEN	Closed to	Embrace
	Different	Diverse
	Views	Perspectives

PARTNER	Loner	Collaborator
	Unreliable	Unifying
	Isolated	Team Player

BRAVE	Risk Averse	Courageous
	Avoid Conflict	Smart
	Avoid Responsibility	Negotiator

ALERT	Distracted	Mindful
	Distant	Focused
	Unsatisfied	Content

DIALOGUE	Uniformed	Informed
	Small Network	Engaged
	Don't Ask	Connected

FAITH	Pessimistic	Optimistic
	Overwhelmed	Resilient
	Dependant	Confident

Appendix 2

De-escalate YOUR stress

Behave Differently

1. Do nothing & allow time to better define your reaction
2. Honestly recognise & manage your emotions
3. Meditate: Breath in reflecting on suffering & breath out reflecting on compassion
4. Prepare your concessions: "If I do this...then will you do that?"
5. Remember we are all one
6. Take a time out to calm down
7. Accept accusations & write them down without reacting

Think Differently

8. Practice non-attachment
9. Recognise the impermanence of both the problem and the solution
10. Recognise others suffer and hurt like you
11. Address their motivational style
12. Be polite, your rudeness and anger returns to you intensified
13. Stop seeing the situation as black or white, right or wrong, look for a middle way
14. Ask "Whose needs are being addressed"
15. Stop thinking me vs. you and think us

Open Dialogue

16. Stop, wait, shut-up and listen
17. Ask other party what you don't know
18. Replace your assumptions, accusations and assertions about others with questions to test the correctness of your views
19. Stop your revenge and ask "how can I help this person overcome their strong emotions?"
20. Apologise & admit mistakes

De-escalate THEIR stress

Behave Differently

21. Show patience to others
22. Demonstrate love for others
23. Be compassionate about their situation
24. Smile at anger and don't let it affect you
25. Work together to define the problem
26. Propose solutions hypothetically ("What if we....?")
27. Encourage polite behaviour and reward it when shown by others
28. Replace your anger with diplomacy

Think Differently

29. Share your thinking about the situation
30. Share why you think the way you do

Open Dialogue

31. Encourage them to talk
32. Don't react, explain you are listening and considering next steps
33. Validate their feelings (e.g. "It's ok that you feel this way about me/the situation")
34. Brainstorm alternative solutions
35. Forgive others genuinely
36. Encourage dialogue amongst stakeholders to explore different perspectives before deciding how best to proceed
37. Ask others about themselves, their thoughts and feelings
38. Spend informal time together
39. Ask others if they are intentionally accusing you and if so to provide examples
40. Use a mediator or facilitator to assist difficult dialogues & those involving a lot of stakeholders

Appendix 3

10 Steps to Project Crisis		10 Steps to Project Success
1. Lack of time allocated		1. Build team
2. Slip behind day by day		2. Get buy in
3. Something goes wrong		3. **Plan project together**
4. Search for cause		4. Preview/prepare for possible crisis
5. Blame each other		5. Get started & manage time
6. Become disorganized		6. **Dialogue regularly**
7. Work overtime to compensate		7. Re-synch as needed
8. Reach breaking point		8. Negotiate changes as they arise
9. Reorganize resources & priorities		9. Work hard
10. Scramble to resolve crisis & complete work		10. Achieve optimal outcome

About the Author

Peter Nixon, BBA MSc, FCPA, specialises in negotiation, dialogue, and business development. He trains, consults, and inspires current and emerging leaders responsible for some of the world's most important dialogues. When the pandemic stopped clients flying him around the world, Peter created **PDI ONLINE** to continue to reach into boardrooms around the world. He has worked with thousands of leaders from over 600 companies, governments, and NGO's in over 60 countries. Peter has published three books on negotiation, dialogue, and business development all of which are available online.

He is a founding course director for the Financial Controllers' Programme (HKICPA) and has taught in Hong Kong (Chinese University (MBA), HKU (Public Health), PolyU, ESF); Canada (McGill, SFU, Bishop's, Champlain Regional College); China (Tsinghua, Fudan, SUFE, UIBE); and Switzerland (Webster). Peter is developing *The Potential Dialogue Centre* to welcome executive team retreats to his family's century old lakeside property in Canada's beautiful Laurentian mountains.

Formative Years

Born during the separatist conflicts in Quebec, Peter quickly learned the importance of dialogue, negotiation, and cultural differences in achieving optimal outcomes for stakeholders. After completing his business studies in Canada, Peter joined Coopers & Lybrand (then Canada's leading firm of audit, tax, and consulting professionals, now called PwC) to audit leading companies in Canada, Switzerland, and Hong Kong. Recognising a need for improved dialogue and negotiation in Asia's rapidly developing economies, Peter launched his consulting and training business in the mid 90's and the rest as they say is history.

Travelling Years

Since launching his business Peter has trained, coached, and consulted thousands of leaders and teams in over 600 companies & governments in 60 countries around the world. Most of Peter's private sector clients include the world's largest banks, professional firms, and MNC's. Public sector dialogues have included: HK-China, Iran-US, Rohingya-Malaysia/Thailand, Israel-Palestine, Aceh-Java, Tibet-China, Sunni-Shia, hostage negotiations, MH370/17, KK Earthquake, development vs preservation debates in Bali, Phuket, Penang, etc.

Recognitions

Peter is the *2019 Asia HR Community Award Winner* in recognition of "his key role in building human capital expertise and high impact individuals and organisations through innovative and pathbreaking consultative work and people engagement". He is still a Fellow of the Hong Kong Institute of CPA's and was a licensed member of the Canadian Institute of CPA's for over 30 years. He has degrees from Bishop's (BBA), McGill (GDPA), and Leicester Universities (MSc) and has also studied at Alberta, Harvard, INSEAD and Fielding. He is a Canadian Chief Scout (1st TMR.), and Knight of Tamara. He has appeared on TEDx, CNBC, Discovery Channel, TV5, TVB, & Media Corp. and showcased globally for YPO and EO. His client collaborations have received awards such as Colgate President's Award (winner), HKMA Training Award (nominee), Top 10 Change Management Consulting Services Companies in APAC (2019, HR Tech Outlook Magazine) and Best Independent Change Management Consultant (2018, HK Business Awards, APAC Insider Magazine).

The Stories

Surviving the democracy protests, trade war and pandemic in Hong Kong is just the latest set of adventures for Peter. He has also been detained in Bahrain, locked up in Tehran, deported from Austria and India, hit by lightning in a small plane north of the Arctic Circle, survived roadside shootings in Aceh, bombings in Pakistan, 7/7 in London, slept with lions in Africa, survived bear intrusions and fought forest fires in Alberta, nearly broke his neck playing ice hockey, meditated with HH the Dalai Lama and Zen monk Thich Nhat Hanh, smuggled a short-wave radio inside the iron curtain and cell phones to Burmese monks, been reminded of the importance of dialogue in Soweto, Auschwitz, Cambodia's Killing Fields, the slums of Colombo, Manila and Bangkok, and witnessed the fire services, healthcare, and teacher strikes during the separatist uprisings in Quebec. Peter has repeatedly joined millions of fellow Hong Kongers marching for democracy, taught students from Tiananmen Square, spent nights with protesters during HK's 2014 Occupy Movement, the Chinese translation of his best-selling book Dialogue Gap is banned by the CCP, and participants were tear-gassed on their way to his dialogue and negotiation talk during Hong Kong's Extradition Bill riots. He has gained inspiration personally watching the world come together at the Olympics, World Scout Jamborees, and World Cup Football and World Cup Rugby. He has led his small business through the ravages of the Pandemic, Democracy Protests, Trade War, Asian Currency Crisis, Bird Flu, SARS, the Great Recession and more. Peter even helped a Palestinian friend buy a camel while surrounded by one million worshippers at India's Pushkar's Mela, an annual pilgrimage thousands of years old where dipping your body into Pushkar Lake during November's full moon (which Peter did) brings eternal salvation (he is still waiting □).

Community Work

Apart from regularly assisting non-profit organisations that request his help, Peter sits on the finance sub-committee and is immediate past Chairman of Discovery Bay International School, Head of Bishop's University Asia Cabinet, and Director of McGill's Martlet Foundation. Following advisory work for both organisations, Peter was a trustee of Outward-Bound HK and a governance committee member of UNICEF HK for many years.

Potential

Until the pandemic shut down, Peter's in-person workshops were popular for their pace, practicality, humour, and engagement and were often rated the best sessions people ever attended. His goal is to achieve the same level of excellence with his on-line workshops. Peter's *Dialogue Puzzle* helps leaders achieve optimal outcomes by ensuring the right people talk about the right issues in the right way, at the right time and in the right space. His books include: **Negotiation: Mastering Business in Asia** (2005, Wiley)*; **Dialogue Gap** ("one of the best business titles published this century" SCMP, Wiley, 2012); **The Business Developer's Playbook** (Taylor-Francis, 2019)*; and **Boomer to Zoomer: Hurdles to being #1** (awaiting publication). Peter is also the creator of the popular *Dialogue Playing Cards* (featured on CX in-flight duty free); the *Dialogue Gap App* (IOS and Android but no longer available).

The **Potential Dialogue Institute** includes leaders that have engaged and/or studied the *Potential Dialogue System* in business, government, the professions, education, healthcare, family business, membership groups, NGO's etc. and who want to stay in touch with best practices and applications from around the world. Peter has been engaged to advise a variety of difficult dialogues including: strategy, team building, mediation, sales, procurement, change management, performance management, pitches, investment, business development, talent management, leadership selection, family business, relocation, succession planning, audit, compliance, legal, religious, political, multi-lateral, bi-lateral, start-ups, leadership development, design, relationships, governance, board of directors, senior leadership team, innovation, diversity & inclusion, tech and more.

Learn more about Peter on TED, YouTube, Amazon or contact him at: LinkedIn, or Peter.Nixon@PotentialDialogue.com.

Author's genealogy

Year	Details
1547	**Henry VIII** dies, succeeded by Edward VI
1548	**Stephen Hopkin's** (see 1620 below) father **Capt. John Hopkins** was born in Coventry, Warwick, and worked as an Elizabethan Bowman https://www.geni.com/people/Capt-John-Hopkins/6000000001155763158
1560	Reformation leads to creation of the Church of Scotland by John Knox who studied with John Calvin in Geneva
1581	**Stephen Hopkins** (see 1620 below) is born in Hampshire, England
1620	**Stephen Hopkins** leaves Britain under rule of James 1st and brings his family to America on the **Mayflower**. Peter's maternal great grand-father, **Dr AR Griffith**, is son of James Griffith and Ellen Randall of Grand Forks, North Dakota. Ellen Randall is grand-daughter of Josiah Smith, direct descendant of **Stephen Hopkins.** https://en.wikipedia.org/wiki/Stephen_Hopkins_(Mayflower_passenger)
1709	**Robert MacMorine** born Dumfries, Scotland, Was a Minister of Nether Marcartney Kirkpatrick-Durham, County of Kirkcudbright. https://familysearch.org/wiki/en/Kirkpatrick-Durham,_Kirkcudbrightshire,_Scotland_Genealogy Peter's paternal grandmother is Ada Rose. Ada's maternal grandmother, Catherine McMorine, is the great-granddaughter of Robert MacMorine.
1714-1830	Rule of Georges' I-II-III-IV in Great Britain
1759	Battle of the Plains of Abraham in Canada, the British win over the French in Quebec City
1776	American Revolutionary War 1775-83 included the USA declaration of independence from Britain July 4th, 1776.
1789	In France, the 14 July revolution overrules feudalism and the French write the world's first charter of human rights.
1809	**William Nixon**, grandfather to Peter's grandfather Frank Nixon, is born in Ireland. No record of when William Nixon arrived in Canada
1812	War of 1812 (UK and British North America vs USA) lasted two years with regular incursions along the Canada - US border including in the Eastern Townships (e.g. Lacolle). Truce eventually led to the agreement of the 49th parallel border Canada and USA share today.
1821	McGill University founded in Montreal
1826	**Alexander Rose**, Peter's paternal grandmother's grandfather, arrives to Canada at Montreal from Scotland
1837-1901	Rule of Queen Victoria begins
1841	British found the colony in Hong Kong
1843	Bishop's University is founded in Lennoxville, Quebec
1849	Capital of Canada, which had been in Kingston 1841-44, is moved from Montreal to Toronto, then to Quebec City and eventually to Ottawa in 1866.

1864	Peter's mother's grand-father, **Dr AR Griffith**, is born in Welland, Ontario, son of James Griffith and Ellen Randall of Grand Forks, North Dakota. See 1620.
1867	Confederation of Canada
1868	**Elizabeth Johnson** is born, mother of Ethel Florence Gear, Peter's maternal grand-mother. Peter wears Elizabeth's wedding ring received in the 1890's from her husband Johnson Henry Gear and gifted to Peter upon death of his grandmother.
1872	Ross family build the first cottage at Lac Des Iles
1886	Peter's grandfather **Frank Nixon**, is born in Waterloo, Quebec, grandson of **William Nixon**.
1894	Peter's maternal great-grandfather, Dr AR Griffith, opens **The Homeopathic Hospital of Montreal** at Sherbrooke and McGill College in Montreal, Quebec.
1895	Peter's grandmother, **Ada Blanche Rose** is born.
1898	Peter's maternal grandmother **Ethel Florence Gear** is born
1899	Party of the century? No one left a record of the party but it must have been good
1901-1910	Rule of Edward VII
1903	Peter's maternal great-grandfather, Dr AR Griffith, builds family **cottage at Lac Des Iles**
1909	Peter's father's uncle, William Nixon's wife and two children are killed at Windsor Station, Montreal in the St Patricks Day railway disaster. All buried at Mt Royal Cemetery in Montreal. Peter's father had only 3 cousins, 2 killed here.
1910-1936	Rule of George V, replaced by Edward VIII who abdicated to marry the love of his life
1912	**Camp Tamaracouta** opens north of Montreal – longest continuously operating scout camp in the world. Peter was a camper, Knight of Tamara and Quartermaster there in the 1970's. Camp ceased regular operations in 2019
1914	Britain goes to war
1916	Jim, Harold, and Hugh Griffith sign up for WWI, Peter's grandfather Jim lies about his age, he is only 17, and joins his brothers in the war
1918	Armistice ends WWI and the 3 Griffith boys return safely to Canada
1923	Peter's father, **Albert John Nixon** is born at home on Marlowe Avenue in Montreal
1927	The Homeopathic Hospital of Montreal moves to Sherbrooke St & Marlowe Avenue
1928	Peter's maternal grand-father, Dr JJ Griffith builds **icehouse at Lac Des Iles**
1929	Peter's mother, **Florence Ann Griffith** is born at The Homeopathic Hospital of Montreal
1929	Peter's maternal grand-father, Dr JJ Griffith builds **cottage at Lac Des Iles**
1932	The Great Depression – Canada is second worst affected country in world after USA
1936	Peter's maternal great grand-father and founder of the Montreal Homeopathic Hospital, **Dr AR Griffith** dies at Montreal Homeopathic Hospital
1936-1952	Rule of George VI
1940	Canada joins WWII
1942	Peter's great uncle, Dr Harold Griffith, uses curare for the first time, a feat that earns him a place in the history of Anaesthesia
1944	Peter's grandfather, **Frank Brigham Nixon** dies and is buried at Mt Royal Cemetery
1945	WW2 ends

1951	Homeopathic Hospital of Montreal renamed ("QEH") **Queen Elizabeth Hospital of Montreal** in honour of Queen Mother wife of George VI
1952	Reign of Queen Elizabeth II begins
1955	Peter's brother **Robert Nixon** born QEH
1958	Peter's brother **David Nixon** born at QEH
1961	**Peter Nixon** born at QEH
1966	Peter's paternal grandmother, Ada Blanche Rose dies, buried Mt Royal Cemetery.
1967	Montreal hosts **Expo '67** World Exposition, Peter's first immersion to world cultures
1968	Peter's maternal grandfather dies, Dr JJ at QEH, buried at Lac Des Iles
1970	FLQ terrorists crisis brings tanks onto the streets of Montreal
1974	Peter becomes a Knight of Tamara and Canadian Chief Scout
1975	Peter attends 14th World Boy Scout Jamboree in Lillehammer Norway together with over 17,000 scouts from 94 countries. Peter's second immersion to world cultures.
1976	Montreal hosts summer Olympics. Peter's third immersion to world cultures.
1976	PQ elected in Quebec and English begin to leave province in droves. Nixon family stay in Montreal because of ties to the Queen Elizabeth Hospital and Lac Des Iles
1980	Quebec Referendum, Federalist NO side wins over separatists with 59.6% of the vote
1981	Peter's scholarship year at U of Alberta
1983	Peter's maternal grandmother, Ethel Florence Gear dies at Rawdon, Quebec and is buried at Lac Des Iles. Peter's mother inherits Lake cottage
1983	Peter graduates from Bishop's University
1984	Peter joins "Big 8" firm Coopers & Lybrand after a year sabbatical to learn French and study accounting at McGill
1987	Peter graduates from McGill University
1988	Peter engages Marie Marchand from Quebec City and together they move to Geneva, Switzerland
1988	Peter completes his Chartered Accountancy designation
1989	Peter & Marie marry in Geneva and move to Hong Kong
1989	Mergers reduce the Big 8 to the Big 6
1989	The Soviet Union collapses, Berlin Wall opens, Tiananmen Square incident
1992	Peter's daughter **Ni Si Nixon** born, adopted 1993
1993	Peter incorporates Potential Limited
1994	Peter's son **Long Tim Nixon** born, adopted same year
1994	Peter resigns from Coopers & Lybrand in Hong Kong and launches his consulting career
1994	Nelson Mandela released from prison to become President of South Africa for the next five years.
1995	Peter's son **Jean-Pierre Nixon** born
1995	Quebec Referendum – Federalist No side wins over separatists with only 50.6% of the vote
1995	QEH closed by Quebec's separatist government but they blame Federal government provincial transfer budget cuts. Federal government blames OECD indebtedness rules.
1997	Hong Kong returns to Chinese rule June 30th
1997	Asian currency crisis wipes out fortunes in Asia starting July
1998	Bird Flu crisis infects humans for the first time (in Hong Kong)

1998	Montreal suffers worst Ice Storm in history, power cut for up to three weeks in freezing January temperatures. Peter's mother is hospitalised (she never went home), Peter's father catches pneumonia from cold but recovers and meets his eventual sweetheart Patricia at the TMR Town Hall shelter
1998	Big 6 merge again to become the Big Five
1998	Peter's mother Winkie dies, Peter's father inherits Lac Des Iles
1999	Party of the millennium – Peter watched arrival of a new millennium with family and friends in Hong Kong
2001	The Big 5 become the Big 4 after the collapse of Arthur Anderson
2001	9/11 terrorist attacks on World Trade Centre and Pentagon, 3000 killed, 6000 injured, world outlook changes
2002	Bali Bombing – 200 killed, 200 injured
2002	SARs outbreak in Hong Kong, schools closed.
2004	Asian Tsunami kills 280,000 people
2005	Peter publishes ***Negotiation: Mastering Business in Asia***
2005	7/7 bombing in London while Peter and his family are visiting London for the first time. 56 killed, 700 injured. Family unhurt.
2011	Peter visits Vimy Ridge nearly 100 years after his grandfather JJ Griffith was there during WW1 as a stretcher bearer with the Cdn. Expeditionary Force
2012	Peter publishes ***Dialogue Gap***
2013	Peter's father dies, Peter and his two brothers inherit Lac Des Iles
2013	Peter travels to Brazil and South Africa for the first time
2016	Peter travels to New Zealand for the first time
2018	Peter buys cottage from brothers and renames it the **Potential Dialogue Centre**
2019	Peter publishes ***The Business Developer's Playbook***. Hong Kong erupts in protest vs Chinese rule
2020	Coronavirus erupts in China and spreads globally affecting world markets.
2020	Peter publishes ***We're F*cked*** and launches PDI Online, his popular 3-day in-person workshops converted to 5 streams of 6 modules each on YouTube and Zoom

Bibliography

- Bliss, Phillip, *Dare to be a Daniel*, 1873, Bliss apparently wrote the song for his Sunday school class at the First Congregational Church of Chicago, Illinois
- Buckingham, Marcus and Clifton, Donald, *Now Discover Your Strengths*, Free Press, 2001, New York
- Csikszentmihalyi, Mihaly, *Flow: The Psychology of Optimal Experience*, Harper Perennial, New York, 1991
- Fuller, Buckminster, *Operating Manual for Spaceship Earth*, Lars Muller, 1969
- Gittins, Paul *On Track Henry Gittins – Railway Pioneer in Siam & Canada*, River Books, 2014, Bangkok
- Goleman, Daniel, *A Force for Good: The Dalai Lama's Vision for Our World*, Penguin Random House, New York, 2015
- Goleman, Daniel, *Destructive Emotions: A Scientific Dialogue with the Dalai Lama*, Random House, New York, 2003
- Grant, Adam, *Originals,* Viking, 2016 New York
- Hawn, Goldie, *The MindUP Curriculum: Grades PreK–2: Brain-Focused Strategies for Learning—and Living*, The Hawn Foundation, 2011, USA
- Hersey, Paul, Blanchard, Kenneth, Johnson, Dewey, *Management of Organisational Behaviour*, Pearson, 2012
- Hofstede, Geert, *Cultures Consequences: International differences in work related values*, 1980, Sage Publications, California
- Lendrum, Tony, *The Strategic Partnering Handbook*, McGraw-Hill, Australia, 1995
- McRae, John, *In Flanders Fields*, Canadian poet, physician, author, artist, and soldier in World War I. First published in PUNCH magazine in December 1915.
- Myers, Isabel Briggs and Myers, Peter, *Gifts Differing: Understanding Personality Type*, Consulting Psychologists Press, 1980, California
- Nixon, Peter, *Negotiation: Mastering Business in Asia*, Wiley, Singapore, 2005
- Nixon, Peter, *Dialogue Gap: Why Communication isn't enough and what we can do about it fast*, Wiley, Singapore, 2012
- Schumacher, EF, *Small is Beautiful: Economics as if People Mattered*, Blond & Briggs, London, 1973
- Scudder, Tim and Lacroix, Debra, *Working with SDI*, 2013, Personal Strengths Publishing, California
- Seligman, Martin, *Authentic Happiness: Using the New Positive Psychology to Realize Your Potential for Lasting Fulfilment*, Simon & Schuster, New York, 2002
- Shehadeh, Raja *Language of War, Language of Peace Palestine, Israel, and the Search for Justice,* Profile Books, London2015
- Sinek, Simon, *Start with Why: How Great Leaders Inspire Everyone to Take Action*, Penguin, New York, 2009
- Stuart-Kotze, Robin, *Performance: The Secrets of Successful Behaviour*, Pearson Education, Great Britain, 2006
- Tan, Chade-Meng, *Search Inside Yourself: The Unexpected Path to Achieving Success, Happiness (and World Peace)*, HarperCollins, New York, 2012
- Zakaria, Fareed, *In Defence of a Liberal Education*, W. W. Norton & Company, New York, 2015

Keywords

Companies	Places	People	Concepts
ADB	Alberta	Adam Smith	Arab Spring
Barefoot College	Bagan	Aung San Suu Kyi	Blue Book
Big Four	Bahamas	Dan Aykroyd	Brexit
Bishop's	Bahrain	David Cameron	Challenge Mapping
Boy Scouts	Bangkok	Deng Xiaoping	Confucian
Bunker Roy	Beijing	Denise Ho	Cultural Consequence
Carlyle School	Boston	Frank Nixon	Culture
Caterpillar	Brazil	George Ewing	Definition of Culture
CGA Canada	Britain	Goldie Hawn	Equilibrium Point
CLP	Burma / Myanmar	Hersey & Blanchard	Flow
Credit Committee	Cambodia	HH The Dalai Lama	Gini Index
CSL	Chao Phraya River	ISIS	Governing Dynamics
DBIS	Dharamshala	Jean Lesage	Great Depression
Disney	Eastern Europe	Jean-Pierre	Great Recession
Enactus	EU	John Belushi	Hippocratic Oath
EO	Europe	John Nash	Iraq War
Expedia	Fort McMurray	Justin Trudeau	Manama Dialogue
ExxonMobil	Geneva	King George VI	Nobel Prize
Google	German	Lam Wing-Kee	Octopus Card
GSK	Germany	Lee Kuan Yew	Participatory Budgeting
HKCEC	Golden Square Mile	Long Tim	Potentialism
Hofstede	Hong Kong	Margaret Thatcher	PTSD
HP	India	Martin Seligman	Puja
IBM	Israel	Mikhail Gorbachev	SDI
IBM	Japan	Nelson Mandela	Situational Leadership
IDEO	Korea	Ni Si	Strengths Finder
IMF	Kuala Lumpur	Queen Elizabeth I	TBFF
Inland Revenue	Malaysia	Queen Elizabeth II	The 1%
INSEAD	Marlowe Avenue	Rohingya	
Johnson Electric	Melbourne	Ronald Reagan	
KCRC	Montreal	Rudy Giuliani	
Lancôme	New York City	Sir Winston Churchill	
Leaders Quest	Oman	The Blues Brothers	
Lenovo	Ottawa	Umbrella Revolution / Movement	
LinkedIn	Palestine		
Marriott	Peel Street		
MBTI	Penang		
McDonald's	PRC		
McGill University	Qatar		

Montreal Homeopathy	Quebec		
MTRC	Rangoon		
NCDD	Rio Grande do Sul		
Our Singapore Conversation	Samut Prakan		
Philip Morris	Seattle		
PWC	Sechelt		
QE Hospital	Seoul		
RBC	Sherbrook Street		
RSOG	Silicon Valley		
SC Bank	Silvermine Bay		
SIM	Singapore		
Time Magazine	Singapore		
UBER	South Africa		
UNICEF	Soviet Union		
WIS	Taiwan		
YPO / WPO	Tamaracouta Scout Reserve		
	Thailand		
	The Gulf		
	Tiananmen Square		
	Tibet		
	Tokyo		
	UK		
	Victoria BC		
	West Virginia		
	World Trade Centre		

Before the pandemic forced Canadian author, speaker, and international negotiation consultant, Peter Nixon, to lockdown in Hong Kong, he spent most weeks during the last 30 years in dialogue with thousands of leaders from hundreds of organisations in nearly 60 countries worldwide. This unique experience convinced Nixon our current economic, political, and environmental dysfunction was evidence a new direction was needed to continue to thrive on earth throughout the 21st Century.

Offered as an upgrade to the flawed 16th and 17th century economic policies of Adam Smith and Karl Marx, Nixon offers *Potentialism* as the 21st century solution to the age-old conflict between capitalism and socialism. Potentialism requires leaders to dialogue and partner with others to maximise potential instead of corporate profits or government control.

Potentialism is based on the Nobel Prize winning economics of Professor John Nash, made famous in the Ron Howard film, *A Beautiful Mind.* In this timely book, Nixon reminds us to think global, focus on potential, treat the environment as a key stakeholder in all our dialogues, and jump the hurdles holding us back from achieving optimal outcomes in the world today.

www.ingramcontent.com/pod-product-compliance
Lightning Source LLC
Chambersburg PA
CBHW030658220526
45463CB00005B/1830